Adultery

Adultery

Louise DeSalvo

BEACON PRESS   BOSTON

BEACON PRESS

25 BEACON STREET

BOSTON, MASSACHUSETTS

02108–2892

WWW.BEACON.ORG

Beacon Press books are published under the auspices
of the Unitarian Universalist Association of Congregations.
© 1999 by Louise DeSalvo. All rights reserved
Printed in the United States of America

05 04 03 02 01 00 99   8 7 6 5 4 3 2 1

Text design and composition by Julia Sedykh Design

LIBRARY OF CONGRESS CATALOGING-IN-PUBLICATION DATA

DeSalvo, Louise A., 1942–

Adultery / Louise DeSalvo.

p. cm.

ISBN 0–8070–6224–3

1. Adultery. 2. Adultery in literature. I. Title.

HQ806.D47   1999

306.73′6—dc21   99–14814

For Geri Thoma, with thanks

One

Unless you consciously (or unconsciously) want to jet-propel yourself into committing adultery, reading about it isn't such a good idea. Because reading about it, I can assure you, will almost certainly result in your thinking about doing it, and perhaps even in your doing it.

(Dante believed this too. For in the *Inferno* of his *Divine Comedy*, he recounts the story of the beginning of the adulterous affair between Paolo and Francesca. Francesca explains to Dante that one day, while she and Paolo are reading about Lancelot and Guinevere, their erotic desire becomes so uncontrollable that they drop the book and yield to impulse. Francesca explains: "He kissed my mouth all trembling:/A Galeotto was the book, and he who wrote it;/That day we read no further."

And Madame Recamier, best known for her love affair with Chateaubriand, also believed that reading about adultery, even the troublesome variety, caused it to happen for her. When she started reading the novels of Madame de La Fayette [according to Dan Hofstadter in *The Love Affair as a Work of Art*], she observed: "This sort of reading is actually rather dangerous, because it makes the reader accept the struggle between passion and virtue as something natural. . . . Though I did not miss the pleasures of love, I missed the pain. I thought I was made to love and suffer, but I loved nobody and nothing, and suffered only from my own indifference." What to do but to go out and find someone to love so that she could live a life of emotional distress?)

Then after you read about adultery, and after you do it, or think about doing it, you might find yourself writing about it (in your journal, in torrid love letters). You might even write a book about it—a novel, most likely (because you can change the names, disguise the circumstances), or a chapbook of poetry (you can pass the poems off as being about your partner or as poems you wrote years ago about a boyfriend or girlfriend you had in high school). And then perhaps some other on-the-fence-about-adultery person will read your work, and the whole cycle of reading about adultery, and committing adultery, and writing about adultery, will begin all over again.

Louise DeSalvo   *Adultery*

An example of this cycle of reading about adultery, committing adultery, then writing about adultery exists in the life and work of Edith Wharton. Wharton, whose marriage to her husband, Teddy, was a sexual disaster, began an adulterous relationship in her mid-forties with W. Morton Fullerton, an American journalist and intimate friend of Henry James. It was her first passionate love affair. This relationship, though it lasted a short time, taught Wharton much of what she had always wanted to know about the human heart and about the body's capacity for ecstasy and the soul's potential for despair.

Before she met Fullerton, according to one of her biographers, R. W. B. Lewis, the image of "a dream-ridden woman trapped in an unhappy marriage" in Gustave Flaubert's *Madame Bovary* had captured Wharton's imagination. So too had the unconventional and passionate sex life of the writer George Sand, especially as it had been described in her *Histoire de ma vie*. Wharton made a pilgrimage to Sand's country house, Nohant, during a motor tour of France. In seeing the place where Sand had lived, where Sand had loved, Wharton believed that she might capture something of Sand's free-spirited nature. Her behavior with Fullerton was, in part, patterned upon that of Sand, though Wharton herself could never manage Sand's emotional insouciance. (Years later, though, Fullerton described her as an uninhibited erotic sister to George Sand, so Wharton appears to have learned *something* from Sand.)

Wharton read, too, the novels and letters of Hortense Allart, a little-known nineteenth-century French novelist, whose robust adulterous life—Chateaubriand and Bulwer-Lytton were among her numerous lovers—Wharton admired even more than her works. But it was Allart's sexually explicit letters that most fascinated her. Henry James, Wharton's friend and confidant, confessed that he couldn't understand Wharton's interest in Allart's endless descriptions of "copulations." Where else, though, could Wharton learn of such matters? Wharton's social position precluded the possibility of her learning what she wanted to know about sex through conversation. And Henry James surely was in no position to answer her questions about eroticism. So it was precisely Allart's detailed renderings that Wharton relished.

She had no model in her life, other than literary ones, for a woman who obeyed her sexual desire. When she married, Wharton was almost entirely sexually ignorant. As Lewis reports in his biography, when she gathered courage to ask her mother "what marriage was really like," her mother impatiently answered, "I never heard such a ridiculous question!"

After Wharton and Fullerton began their adulterous affair, Wharton took him on a pilgrimage to see Allart's home in Herblay. That evening, she wrote a sonnet called "Ame Close," which she referred to as her "Herblay sonnet," to commemorate their visit to her adulterous idol's home and their complex and compromised passion.

Gloria C. Erlich, in "The Libertine as Liberator" (*Women's Studies 20*, no. 2 (1991): 97–108) describes how, at forty-five years of age, Wharton was introduced to Fullerton through Henry James. She was, at the time, actively seeking love, for she had been living in an "emotionally stagnant" marriage that would soon end with an emotionally disturbed, adulterous man. Fullerton, at forty-two, had just ended a marriage to a French singer, and had become engaged to an adoptive sister. The prospect of an adulterous affair with Wharton appealed to him because "he could indulge his predilection for . . . eroticism without risk of commitment." Wharton seems to have known something about Fullerton's reputation as a sexual gadfly but she apparently didn't know about his engagement. Still, like many others, she relished their "unique, transcendent love."

Their intense, passionate relationship lasted only several months when Wharton moved to Paris in 1908; but they corresponded for the remaining thirty years of Wharton's life. Though brief, the impact of this affair on Wharton lasted a lifetime, for she learned that she was capable of a wanton passion that was, for her, also an intensely spiritual experience. She did not regret the pain she suffered when Fullerton withdrew from her. She understood, too, that it had given her material for a multitude of artistic works. For, as she observed, "Ordinary troubles dry one up; they're as parching as the scirocco; but in every heart there should be one grief that is like a well in the desert."

Wharton understood her love in literary terms. She called him "Friend of my heart," which is what Clelia Conti says to Fabrizio del Dongo when she invites him into her bed in Stendhal's *The Charterhouse of Parma*. She gave him a copy of Flaubert's letters to George Sand, and Benjamin Constant's *Adolphe,* the story of a seducer who is pursued by the woman he abandons.

At first, she claims she was unable to read much after they began their affair. "For the first time in my life," she wrote, "*I can't* read." But this didn't last long. For like so many others, Wharton needed reading to inflame her lust, to ignite her desire.

Soon after their affair began, she was reading voraciously, and about adultery. Paul Marieton's account of George Sand's affair with Alfred de Musset. William Morris's "Defence of Guenevere" for an understanding of how another woman "slip[ped] slowly" into adultery. John Donne's "The Extasie" ("to our bodies turn we then, that so / Weak men on love revealed a look; / Love's mysteries in souls do grow, / But yet the body is his book"). And the works of Nietzsche for his theory of how heeding animal instinct undermined traditional culture and values, and how this was sometimes good and necessary.

After they became lovers, Fullerton told Wharton that their affair would be good for her writing, and, according to her biographer, Shari Benstock, it was. Wharton began writing a love diary, called "The Life Apart," which reads pretty much like anyone else's love diary (yours, mine) would read. "Sometimes I think that if I could go off with you for twenty-four hours to a little inn in the country, . . . I should ask no more." "You . . . have given me the only moments of real life I have ever known." "I appear to myself like a new creature opening dazzled eyes on a new world."

And like many another foolish lover, she told Fullerton how much she needed him, and she gave her diary to him to read. He learned that she was so smitten with him that he had the upper hand in their relationship. This hastened its end, for Fullerton preferred his lovers to be unavailable, unobtainable, which is why he initially chose the married Wharton.

Wharton wrote letters to Fullerton which read pretty much like anyone else's love letters, especially the pained ones written when it becomes obvious to her that, although he might be the most important man in her life, she is but one of many women in his. "If when you hold me, and I don't speak, it's because all the words in me seem to have become throbbing pulses, and all my thoughts a great golden blur." "Sometimes I feel that I *can't* go on like this." "Yesterday, in my despair, I very nearly cabled you the one word: *Inconsolable*." "You woke me from a long lethargy." "If I could lean on *some feeling* in you—a good and loyal friendship, if there's nothing else!—then I could go on."

Of course, there was poetry. She wrote about him in a sonnet series called "The Mortal Lease." She wrote about him, too, in fiction, in stories exploring her favorite themes of the entrapment of a woman in marriage, thwarted desire, and lifelong yearning for something unknown and unattainable. In "The Choice" (about an adulterer who wants her husband to die but whose lover dies instead); "The Letters" (based on their correspondence); "The Pretext" (about his infidelity to her); and, ultimately, in the novels *The Custom of the Country* and segments of *The Mother's Recompense*.

Reading about adultery is dangerous. But writing about adultery also has its perils. For let's say that instead of doing it (committing adultery, that is), you decide to write about it, without doing it, as Robert

James Waller did when he wrote *The Bridges of Madison County*, to channel your illicit desire.

After Waller wrote the novel (which launched, I suspect, scores of affairs between middle-aged farm women and cigarette-smoking, boot-wearing, camera-toting Robert Kinkaid wanna-bes), Waller found *himself* in the middle of an affair with the woman who worked for him as a landscaper and handyman. It ended his thirty-five-year marriage.

Or maybe, like Sylvia Plath, or like Henry Miller, your marriage has broken up because your husband or your wife has had an affair and decided to leave you. You write about it, you can't stop yourself from writing about it. You write enraged poems, as Plath did, about your husband's behavior and his abandonment. Searing poems. Angry poems. Poems like "The Other," "Burning the Letters," "For a Fatherless Son," "A Birthday Present." Poems that explore the suicidal despair that all too often follows adultery's betrayal.

Writing about adultery like Plath did is dangerous; it might even be deadly. For dwelling on the fact of betrayal can make you feel worse, not better. It helped propel Plath into her final suicidal despair; it might have even hastened the end of her life.

Perhaps you plan a novel, or two, or more—like Henry Miller's *Crazy Cock* or *Tropic of Cancer* or *The Rosy Crucifixion*—about how your wife has left you, and you write about this your whole writing life. You think that this is helpful; you believe that it has healed the greatest psychic wound you've ever suffered. Still, because you're always writing about the woman who deserted you, you can't seem to find another woman beautiful enough, sexy enough, commanding enough, to replace her. At the end of your life, you are still writing about her. At the end of your life, she still holds you in thrall. You realize that, because you've written about her your whole life, you've loved her your whole life.

Writing about someone, then, might help you get over a love affair. But it can also keep you bound to a lost lover.

Annette Lawson, in her definitive *Adultery: An Analysis of Love and Betrayal,* discovered, to my mind, something wondrous. That many of the people she talked to for her study (adulterers, all living in England during the 1980s) said that their decision to embark upon their infidelities had been greatly influenced by the books and other writings (like magazine articles) that they had read. What they were reading mattered more than their upbringing!

Gustave Flaubert knew this. For in his novel *Madame Bovary,* the properly raised Emma's reading about "love, lovers, sweethearts, persecuted ladies fainting in lonely pavilions. . . and. . . gentlemen brave as lions, gentle as lambs, virtuous as no one ever was, always well dressed and weeping like fountains" leads her into clandestine love.

And what had Lawson's subjects read? Not the Gothic romances Emma Bovary preferred. The works most frequently cited may surprise you. For the infidelities described in the novels most frequently mentioned (except, perhaps, for *Lady Chatterley's Lover*) aren't Harlequin romances. Neither are the love affairs especially romanticized or idealized. In fact, many of them turn out to be downright awful.

What the women had read were the novels of D. H. Lawrence (especially, of course, *Lady Chatterley's Lover*); those of Margaret Drabble, Fay Weldon, and Rosamond Lehmann; Marilyn French's *The Women's Room;* and the (nonfiction) sexual study of Shere Hite.

For the men: the novels of D. H. Lawrence and Fyodor Dostoyevsky; the works of Freud, Jung, Havelock Ellis, Albert Ellis, and (though I can't imagine why), Alvin Toffler's *Future Shock* and *The Third Wave*.

(No one, it seems, mentioned Nathaniel Hawthorne's *The Scarlet Letter*.)

American readers, contemporary readers, of course, would choose different books. The dangerous book, for me—some years ago, I confess—was Virginia Woolf's *Orlando*. A friend to whom I once admitted this, suggested that it was surely Woolf's satiric detail about the cucumbers growing to absurd lengths during Victorian England that probably did it. Perhaps. But I believe that it was Orlando's equation with living a full life and taking a lover, or several lovers, that did it.

" 'Life! A Lover!' not 'Life! A Husband!' " Orlando cries, and Woolf tells us that (in mockery of her own polygamous lover Vita Sackville-West, upon whom the character is based) "it was in pursuit of that aim that she had gone to town and run about the world."

Certainly, the way to start an affair is to read about one. The path to becoming a paramour (or into an intended paramour's bed) might very well be through a discussion of a book about sex or about adultery.

Monica Lewinsky sends Bill Clinton a copy of *Vox.* Which was, considering her motives, an excellent choice, I can assure you, if you yourself haven't read the book. For although *Vox* has been simplistically described by journalists (who probably haven't read it) as "about telephone sex," it is a superb and ironic critique of the depersonalization of eroticism in our time. Paradoxically, it's also very erotic (and not in the least pornographic—and I, for one, have no trouble telling the difference between the two, which doesn't necessarily mean that I am a critic of pornography).

I will admit that I spent one compelling night on my sofa in my study, while my husband was away on a business trip, reading *Vox* when it first came out. And being titillated beyond what I ever thought possible by the very good telephone sex in that book, something that I myself hadn't yet (unfortunately) experienced, though I had surely had my share of "hot" though anxiety-ridden telephone conversations. (I grew up in the days of the party line, and I still assume that every telephone conversation I have is either being overheard by someone or recorded by someone. A few times in my life, I haven't cared. Given recent events, it's an attitude I'm glad I've retained.)

The night I read *Vox*, I even went so far as to flip through my Rolodex for a few maniacal minutes looking for a few men (married, unmarried, it didn't really matter) to call. For telephone sex? No. To set up an actual, hands-on, belly-to-belly assignation, if you want to know the God's honest truth. I had a few candidates in mind. I can assure you that if I used their names here, they would be shocked to learn that they were ever the object of my "venomous lust," to borrow the phrase Henry Miller uses to refer to a lust other than his own. *I* was shocked to discover that they had become the objects of my desire.

Fortunately (or unfortunately) for me, no one I called answered the phone. And I knew better than to leave a breathy message. And so, what did I do after this hypersexualized experience? I went to sleep and dreamed adultery dreams. They were (perhaps) better than the real thing would have been; they surely got me in much less trouble.

Exactly what Bill Clinton did after he read *Vox* (if he read *Vox*) I have not as yet learned, though I feel sure that I soon will learn this and much that I want (or don't want) to know. (I don't mind telling you that I *do* like knowing that Monica Lewinsky told Linda Tripp that she used her affair with Bill Clinton to get over an affair she was having with some guy named Andy who lived on the West Coast. Imagine. Using the President of the United States to get over someone else. What chutzpah! This Andy was *also* married, and I wondered how *he* felt when he found this out, and whether his wife knew, and how she felt, and whether they're still married.)

And what was my husband reading before he started *his* affair? Why, the James Bond novels of Ian Fleming, of course. And how could his life—working every other night and every other weekend as an intern and living with a new baby and a depressed wife on very little money—compare with that of James Bond?

But if he couldn't be 007, he could, at least, fuck around like 007.

The cycle seems to go something like this.

You read a book about adultery. Maybe you stumble into reading it. Maybe you seek it out to juice up your life. You start reading the book and it captures your fancy. You find this curious. Still, there is something about the book that grabs you. You become obsessed by it and can't put it down. You try to read it whenever you can, ignoring the sexual signals your partner may be sending your way. ("Not tonight," you may even say, as you turn your back to her or to him, and clutch your pillow, and continue reading.) Reading about clandestine sex is ever so much more exciting than having sex with a familiar partner.

You tell your friends about the book; you insist that they read it; you even buy a copy for your best friend. You want to talk about the book more than anyone wants to hear you talk about it. When you tell your partner about it (for you do tell your partner about it), her or his eyes glaze over or they look at you strangely. (This should be a danger signal to them, but sometimes they're too wrapped up in their own life to notice.)

Soon you begin to measure your own humdrum life against the passionate and dangerous life depicted in the novel. The clandestine meetings, the risky phone calls (with the partner in the next room). The fabulous sex (positions you haven't tried; acts you haven't performed; places you haven't used for the act of fornication). The intimacy (eyes locking, fingers touching or brushing, tongues licking). And you find your life wanting.

Suddenly, you find your partner boring, and her or his heretofore little endearing habits (the way he sucks his teeth, the way she twirls her hair) revolting. You find yourself unfulfilled. Your job sucks. Your life sucks. Your clothes suck. You need a complete makeover. A lifestyle change.

You realize that you've never lived fully, or freely, or completely, or erotically (whether or not you have, in fact, lived fully, freely, completely, or erotically). No. You've done what you're supposed to do, what your parents programmed you to do, what your partner wants you to do. You've never done what *you* want to do. Not once. Not ever. Hell, you don't even know what you want to do.

Unless you begin to find out soon, you tell yourself, you may as well not bother trying. Life is passing by too quickly. You're twenty-five, or thirty-five, or forty-five, or fifty-five, whatever. You tell yourself that you don't have that much more time left, so you better start living life to the fullest. Now. After all, you only have one life to live, and this one isn't a dress rehearsal.

Everything that, a few days before, seemed wonderful (your partner, your home) and meaningful (your life together, your job) and adorable (your kids, the dog, the cats, the guppy—well, maybe not the guppy, who has always had this terrible habit of shitting long strands while you're having your dinner), everything that, at the very least, you thought was bearable and tolerable (the condition of marriage), now seems trivial and meaningless: a compromise, a trap, even.

You feel caged. You feel suffocated. You need to find a way to get out of this cage. Soon. Now. You want romance in your life. You need romance in your life to come alive. Without it, you will continue to feel dead inside. This is, you tell yourself, the first day of the rest of your life.

A couple of days later, you see someone you know, someone you may have been introduced to once or twice before, maybe someone you work with, and that person suddenly looks different, has an aura, where previously the person was just someone else you worked with or for. And (if you're a woman), before you know it, you're batting your eyes, and tossing your hair, and making very many trips past his desk to the bathroom, and you're wagging your ass a lot more than usual on the way there, and you can't believe you're doing it, because this isn't at all like you, and he notices you. Or (if you're a man), you're puffing out your chest, you're exaggerating your gestures (and knocking things over as you do so), and you're laughing louder than you've ever laughed before ("Har, har, har," you hear yourself chortling in response to some idiot's stupid joke at the water cooler which just happens to be situated close to her workstation), and she notices you.

You meet for lunch. You talk. You lock eyes. She patterns your movements; you pattern hers. You repeat the above behavior a few times or a great many times. You tell him (or her) that you've never felt like this before, that this has never happened to you before (and you believe it). You tell him or her that you like the way you feel, that you don't like the way you feel, that this scares you, that you really don't want to change your life, that you really respect your husband/wife/partner and you wouldn't want to hurt them.

You debate the pros and the cons. You can't shut this off, even though you won't let this overtake your life. Suddenly, you know what to do. You can compartmentalize this relationship, you tell yourself, keep it in its proper place. After all, you're grown-ups, not kids, and you can control yourselves.

Finally, you arrange a meeting. At her place (when her partner is traveling on business) or at your place (when yours is) or at a motel or hotel that is about three-quarters of an hour away from where you work.

Louise DeSalvo *Adultery*

Maybe you go to a business conference. Maybe you yield to impulse.

The sex is fantastic, or great, or good, it doesn't really matter, because it's the thrill of what you're doing that you're not supposed to be doing that's really so fantastic.

Soon, you discover that it's not the sex that glues this thing together, it's *the talking about sex*—about whether you're going to have it, about when you're going to have it, about how good it's going to be when you can have it, about how good it was the last time you had it, about whether you should stop having it, about how you can't stop having it (even though you're not having it all that often), about whether you can live without having it.

If you're smart, you only say these things to each other face to face (preferably after requesting a full body search of the other person to see that there are no hidden microphones). You do not whisper these things on anyone's message machine. You do not send e-mails. You do not write letters. You do not keep a love diary in which you sound like a moron (as Edith Wharton did after she started her affair with Morton Fullerton). You do not write a memoir (as Louise "Ludovica" Pradier did—she was Gustave Flaubert's sometime lover, and he cribbed parts of her story for *Madame Bovary*).

In short, you control yourself. You try to act reasonably. You try not to leave a paper trail. You try not to leave an auditory trail. Still, there are a few lapses. You tell her or you tell him that if anyone asks whether you've done anything, to deny it. Unless you're stupid enough to confess, no one will know.

Still, you sometimes realize that many people will learn exactly what you said and what you did. Your lover, in a moment of boasting, will tell one person, and they will tell a few, and those few will tell a few, and so on, and pretty soon, thousands of people who don't even know you will know. (Remember the lessons you learned in mathematics about geometric progression.) You repress this.

(Remember, please, to make a full disclosure of whatever illicit moments there have been in your private life, no matter how insignificant they may seem to you, before running for public office. Realize that, as Kinsey observed, people who know your private business won't talk about it publicly unless they have a political reason or a vengeful reason to do so. Realize that, as Kinsey observed, even if they have done the same kind of thing themselves, *especially if* they have done the same kind of things themselves, they won't be empathic toward your transgressions. If you point out to them that they are as flawed as you are, they will accuse you of blackmail.)

Louise DeSalvo *Adultery*

Adultery stories have a life of their own. They are passed from person to person. They are traded like precious baseball cards. People would rather hear an adultery story than hear about the stock market, war, drought, pestilence, plague, the destruction of the ecosystem. Rome did not burn as Nero fiddled. Rome burned as Nero listened to a story about who was doing what to whom.

Although people begin their adulteries to take control of their lives, to author their own existence, people, you must understand, almost always eventually lose control of their adultery stories and they lose control of their lives because of their adultery stories. As my husband has lost control of his adultery story. As Bill Clinton has lost control of his adultery story and, it seems, lost control of his life.

Other people take possession of the narrative. The narrative becomes public coin.

Because of this inevitable fact, there are many potential denouements—so many, in fact, that it would be a mistake to try to list them all. They do, however, fall into a few general categories.

The adultery that ends tragically. This variation is the most common and it entails discovery, disgrace, the breakup of families, the end of presidencies, and possibly even death—murder and/or suicide. It is the kind most commonly found in fiction—William

Styron's *Lie Down in Darkness;* Kate Chopin's *The Awakening,* for instance. But it happens all too often in life, as it did in that of Sylvia Plath.

Here's a tragic adultery story I witnessed: he moves out of his house; she moves out of hers. They leave their children behind. They set up house together; they buy nice furniture, and rugs, and plants. Their kids' pictures are affixed to the refrigerator in the kitchen. They miss their kids. They miss them a lot. When you visit them, though, this love nest smells of despair. One day, for whatever reason, he can't take it anymore. He takes all the pills from the medicine cabinet, swallows them, goes into the kitchen, takes the butcher knife and stabs himself in the heart. When she comes home, she finds him. There is blood everywhere, even on the pictures of their children.

The adultery that, while it lasts, seems not to damage the marriage of either party, that does not end either marriage, perhaps because the adulterous couple have been smart enough to keep their mouths shut. The adultery, though, has unpredictable unfavorable future consequences.

(He has always believed that he needed a relationship beyond his marriage, though he has never admitted his twenty year affair to his wife that began before the birth of their only child. His daughter, he thinks, has probably learned of his clandestine affair. Perhaps one evening, when his wife was out and his daughter was in bed, and (he thought) asleep, and she over-heard him on the telephone. Can this be the reason that, at seventeen, his formerly charming offspring has become sullen and withdrawn and refuses to speak to him? Why she walks out of the room whenever he walks into it? Why she calls him a "million-dollar phony"? Why she refuses to go to college? Nothing else can explain it.)

(She has had one torrid affair that was soon over when she was in her mid-thirties and her son was four years old. Though she thought of ending her mar-riage, she didn't, and she never told her husband about her experience. The affair only lasted a few months, though her friendship with the man lasted much longer, but during those months, her behavior was erratic and unpredictable. Afterward, she suffered a deep depression for which she sought counseling. Now her son is in his mid-thirties, and he has confessed to his mother that *he* is having a torrid affair and that he is thinking of leaving his wife and their four-year-old child. Is history, she asks, repeating itself? Did her behavior lead to his?)

There is *the adultery that ends equivocally* (as Lady Chatterley's does—we aren't sure, at the novel's end, whether the lovers will reunite.)

Then *there is the adultery that ends happily enough* as mine did, as the adultery in Sloan Wilson's *The Man in the Grey Flannel Suit* did, as the adultery in Robert

James Waller's *The Bridges of Madison County* did (though about this, there is some dispute).

Kinsey insists there are more adulteries that end happily enough than you think. But these stories don't often get written down. They're not dramatic enough. They are not a part of the popular mythology of adultery in our culture. For, as Kinsey observed, people who have themselves engaged in adulterous relationships are reluctant to talk openly about them, even if they are promised anonymity, for they know that adultery is almost always condemned when it becomes publicly acknowledged. This, Kinsey speculated, is because of the underlying puritanical strain in American culture, and also because of a deep-seated hypocrisy about sex that seems to run deep in American life. For Kinsey discovered that even people who themselves had experienced adultery, or who had no private moral misgivings about committing the act, would rebuke the acts of others.

Once, in the eighties, I tried publishing a novel in the United States called *Casting Off* that spoofed people's responses to adultery—it had been published in England. In the narrative, there were two women, both married, both polygamous. Neither ends her marriage; neither gets discovered. The book was based upon my interviews with a score of adulterous women who lived all over the United States, who were happy to share their stories so long as I disguised the details in my work.

Editors were almost universally outraged by the book. "This can't happen!" It happens all the time, I replied. "Can you kill one of them off?" Well, no. I think it's important that their lives aren't destroyed, and that they survive, even flourish. "Totally unrealistic." Would you like to talk to the woman I talked to in Iowa? Maybe it was the same woman that Waller talked to in writing *The Bridges of Madison County*. "Immoral." Well, it depends on what you call moral. "Perverse." Yes, certainly.

After the publication of Waller's *Bridges,* a reviewer for the *Los Angeles Times* ranted that the book was "pornography for middle-aged women" that carried the dangerous message that "affairs are not devastating to marriage, to children." Times, it seems, haven't changed.

Then there is the *retaliatory adultery story.* As in Nora Ephron's *Heartburn* (which attacks her ex-husband). As in Flaubert's *Madame Bovary* (which attacks his lover Louise Colet, among others, as Colet's biographer Francine du Plessix Gray points out). As in Henry Miller's entire life's work (which traduces his wife, June, for abandoning him for her female lover).

Even Virginia Woolf wrote one of these in her first

novel, *The Voyage Out*. Her portrait, in that novel, of Richard Dalloway was surely inspired by her relationship with her sister Vanessa's husband, Clive Bell, after Vanessa gave birth to her first child. It might only (only?) have been a highly charged affair that probably included what we would today call "heavy petting."

Whether the affair was sexual or not, we really don't know, but Woolf believed that it affected her profoundly her entire life, and she continued to write adultery into her fiction throughout her career. Her flirtation, or whatever it was, with her brother-in-law drove a wedge between her and her sister and it made Woolf feel worthless. During its aftermath, Woolf became seriously suicidal.

The most important moment in *The Voyage Out* is when a married man—Mr. Dalloway—kisses a young woman—Rachel Vinrace. Now, you might not call that adultery. I don't. But some people do. What's clear in the novel, though, is however little Dalloway did, he had adultery on his mind. Now, although Dalloway seems to have had no problems with this act, he does blame Rachel (a stand-in for Woolf) for tempting him and, according to some critics (myself included), it actually *kills her*.

But what interests me most, because I am fascinated by how often vengeful portraits of ex-lovers show up in works of art, is how savagely Woolf satirizes Dal-

loway, whose character is based upon her ex-lover.
He is an insufferable bore; a sanctimonious hypocrite;
a self-satisfied moron. What particularly annoyed
Woolf during her relationship with Clive Bell were
the tendentious mini-lectures he delivered to her
about the function of art and the criticisms he made of
her novel-in-progress. In her novel, Woolf perfectly
captures his self-satisfied high-mindedness. In their
personal interactions, Woolf was rarely hypercritical
of Clive Bell, but in her fiction, she spoke her mind.

I am interested in *adultery stories* and in thinking
about the very significant role adultery stories play in
our lives. I like to think about how and why people
tell adultery stories to one another (for telling one is
always risky) and also why we listen to them and read
them and write them and rewrite them. Recently, it
seems the whole world has stopped whatever it's doing
to listen to the Clinton/Lewinsky adultery story—
and what a story it is.

Sometimes I think that the only reason we *have*
affairs is so that we will have a completely new story
to tell ourselves about who we are, and so that we
will have a completely new, startling, and (we think)
exciting story to tell others about ourselves, a story
that will show others that we're not who we were.
For doesn't an adultery story transform our image of
a person?

I have adultery on my mind because we know
a lot about adultery and because we know nothing
about it at all; because we know why people do it
and because we have no idea at all why people do it;
because we know how many people do it and because
we have no idea how many people do it; because
adultery is both an institution and because it's not;
because it's private and it's public; because everyone
wants to know about it and no one wants to hear
about it; because it's exciting and it's dull; because
there are rules that go along with having an affair
and because it's also anarchic and it breaks the rules;
and because most fundamentally, it threatens the
institution of marriage even as it helps to maintain it.

Adultery/marriage—flip sides of the same coin.
Without the possibility of infidelity, would many
of us marry and go about the business of setting up
households and (sometimes) having children and
rearing them? Honestly (and who, after all, is honest
about adultery), I suspect that I would not have.
Imagining myself bound to one person for the rest
of my life without the escape valve that adultery provides would have surely kept me single.

I like to think about adultery because it's enigmatic
and puzzling and complicated and because an adultery
story is *always* about much more than sex and marriage and fidelity and infidelity. It's *always* a story that
tries to discover the relationship between what we

desire and who we are; between what we want and what we need; between what we have and what we don't have and how that drives us. An adultery story is always about yearning and loss. And about desire and the freedom to enact one's desire, so that an adultery story is also always about autonomy. And about sorrow. Because in every adultery story, no matter how euphorically it begins, we always encounter more sorrow than we dreamed possible, for adultery always causes sorrow, even as it unfurls whatever past sorrows we have experienced.

An adultery story always tries to determine whether we are in control of our own desire or whether these feelings are beyond our ability to manage them. And these—yearning, loss, desire, sorrow, autonomy— are, at least in my experience, the fundamental bedrock of the chastened human soul.

About ten years after my husband told me that he was having an affair and was thinking of leaving me and our infant son, I awakened in the middle of the night, crept out of bed quietly (so as not to disturb him), went into the kitchen, and started baking corn muffins. I took up a pad of yellow paper and started, too, to write an adultery story of my own, a retaliatory adultery narrative, although I didn't realize it then. After it was completed and, perhaps, published, my husband, if he chose to read it, would never know whether it was a work of the imagination, or whether it was based upon my own experience.

It was four o'clock in the morning, and an unlikely time for baking but not, perhaps, an unlikely time for writing about adultery. The house was still, our two sons were asleep upstairs, and I had been having the most wonderful erotic dream, not about my husband.

I will not bother telling you what was happening in this dream. Writing it down would make it seem far more foolish and far less pleasurable than my experience of it. Since you yourself have no doubt had such a dream, you can, therefore, surely imagine what mine was about. I will therefore spare you the details. All I will say is that what I was very much enjoying took place in an apartment in the meat-packing district of New York City, that I was doing something I don't ordinarily do with my husband, and that, in the dream, it was raining, that I had come into that apartment breathless, drenched to the skin, my body luscious and lubricious (I see I must restrain myself here) under the white shirtwaist dress I was wearing, and that I wasn't wearing any underpants.

In my dream I had, of course, forgotten my umbrella, which is why I had gotten wet. This was something that, in waking life, I never would have done. In real life, I would have checked the weather forecast before going into New York, both in the *New York Times* in the morning and then, again, on WINS 1010 radio just before I was ready to leave. In real life, I would have had my umbrella; I would have had my raincoat; I would have been wearing something dark and sensible if it had been raining; and I most assuredly would have been wearing underpants.

Sometimes (and I was in my mid-thirties at the time), I'd still dream of Roy, the boy I'd loved in high school. In my dreams of him, we never age. We are both still seventeen, the age when last we met. In my dreams, he is still my one, my only true love, though in waking life, I surely love my husband, must love him, for by now we are married some seventeen years or more, and have gone through so much together, and I've never cheated on him, not really, and we've tried hard, and succeeded, in repairing a marriage that was nearly shattered so soon after it had begun.

In my dreams of Roy, we make love, as we once did, out of doors, under harvest moons, and on wet grass. Or in darkened basement rooms adjoining rooms where our friends are having parties. Or in cars in parking lots after basketball-away games. Or on a ledge of the Palisades overlooking New York City.

On the frequent mornings of these frequent sweet dreams that I have of Roy, I linger long in bed while my husband rises to make our coffee, awaken our children, search the kitchen for something for us to share for breakfast, feed the cats, and let the dog outside to shit and pee. In time, when the clatter in the kitchen can no longer be ignored, I rise, reluctantly, and leave my bed, and kiss my husband good morning, and kiss my children good morning.

On this night, however, the subject of my dream was not my adolescent lover Roy, but an unrecognizable Italian man, about my own age or somewhat younger, who vaguely resembled a photograph of my grandfather, the one who always went to Italy without my grandmother, when he was a young man.

Something in the nature of this dream signaled trouble. So I knew I had to do something domestic quickly. Which is why I started the convection oven. Which is why I dragged out my worn copy and stained copy of *The Joy of Cooking*. Which is why I started making corn muffins at four o'clock in the morning.

But while the corn muffins were cooking (and by now they were browning nicely with perfectly formed little crowns on top, which meant that, distracted though I may have been, I had mixed them perfectly), I found a pad of yellow lined paper, and my favorite pen, and I started writing fiction, something I hadn't ever done before.

What I found myself writing that night (or morning, actually), while my corn muffins were baking, was this:

Louise DeSalvo   *Adultery*

silken bodies of younger and more sexually active men than their hard-pressed, hard-working, upwardly mobile husbands.

She watched her cornmeal muffins rising, rising, perfectly formed, a solace to her children on the morning of the day when she would put on her hat and her coat, grab the express bus in to the Port Authority in New York, and meet that younger man who had been described to her some time ago as sexually voracious. It now sounded very, very good to her, although she confessed to herself that at the time she had been horrified.

As she walked to the bus station, she saw an old woman in the arms of her daughter being carried— dragged, really—up the stairs and into her house. Helen looked away. Not that the image was painful to her, but for a moment the fact that she was on her way into New York City to see this man at the same time that this old woman was just barely managing to negotiate a flight of stairs filled her with a sense of herself 40 years from now, being helped up her own stairs by one of her own children. And would she guess then that the younger woman hurrying past with such energy and purpose was on her way to a day of joy and exquisite bliss? Would she remember?

The last time she had gotten involved, Helen had made sure that it was with a discreet, three-piece-wearing tax accountant with a wife and five children in the sub- urbs, whose idea of infidelity was to drink endless cups of

Louise DeSalvo   *Adultery*

*The day before Helen MacIntyre began to have her
second affair, she got up in the middle of the night to make
her children cornmeal muffins for breakfast. She figured
it was the least that she could do for them. Somewhere
in the corridors of her memory, she remembered reading
a* Woman's Fellowship Cookbook *in which muffins
were embarrassingly and fatuously referred to as "love
bundles."*

*Although she certainly didn't count herself among
those foolish women who would have referred to cornmeal
muffins as "love bundles," nonetheless, any time Helen
MacIntyre had even begun to contemplate the possibility
of having another love affair, she found herself awakening in the middle of the night, unable to resist the
impulse to combine a cup of this, a jigger of that, and
to sit in the silent kitchen with yesterday's* New York
Times, *hearing the reassuring sound of her convection-
turbo oven starting up, which always reminded her of
a jumbo jet turning its engines and which always gave her
a feeling of power and potency, as if she herself could
fly here, jet there, on a moment's notice.*

*She thought about how long it had taken her to appre-
ciate sensation, about how preoccupied she had been for
all those long years with all those substitutes for eroticism
that women find in women's magazines, substitutes de-
signed to keep their hands occupied with knitting needles
and with wool, instead of roving, roving over the silent*

cappuccino opposite her at a fancy midtown restaurant
at lunchtime. Nice and safe. Nice and companionate.
The illusion of adultery without the risk.

He would talk about his children; she would talk
about hers. He would talk about his foreign investments;
he would give her advice about starting hers. He would
talk about his wife and her sexual inadequacies; she
would sigh and stare at the dregs of her coffee and won-
der whether he would ever reach slowly, slowly across
the table to touch her face and stroke her hair.

The only erotic thing that they had ever done together
was to fornicate desperately and quickly one evening on
the top of his desk amid tax forms and debentures, but
that was largely because he wasn't going to see her for the
three months that Helen would be in England that sum-
mer, and she had brought a bottle of wine up to his office
at closing time.

Now that really was something, she had thought deli-
ciously to herself when it was over. Now that was adultery
in the truest sense of the word and it was wonderful. But
it was no harbinger of things to come. As soon as Helen
returned in September, they resumed their routine of cap-
puccino and sympathy, a rather banal and boring substi-
tute for what she had come to regard as the real thing.

Actually it had all started this time, she thought, because
of John Travolta. For when she saw John Travolta in
his white suit, dancing, dancing amid the flashing lights

and pulsing sounds, something within her surfaced, and all she could do was smile with imbecility and sink back into her seat, hoping that no one around her could see her lips part and moisten and her hips thrust forward involuntarily, in the first genuine moment of wantonness and lust that she had experienced in her adult life.

A few days after that, Helen made her first lasagna, and served it to her family with a blank smile. The children looked at her puzzled, because she had told them, many times, that she didn't like pasta and that she wouldn't cook it for them. They wondered if she was having a midlife crisis because she had also been very generous recently and had taken them to see Saturday Night Fever four nights in a row.

But her time had come now. At last.

In her more rational moments—and she was having fewer and fewer of those the closer she was getting to her fortieth birthday—she realized that she had been pushed over the brink this time because her son had become a vegetarian. In a peculiar way that only another woman would understand, it was that, and not her husband's string of infidelities, which had been the very last straw, the one that broke down her resistance and cast her, once again (but in the real sense this time) into that group of women that she had read about but never, in her earlier years, dreamed of joining—Molly Bloom, Anna Karenina, Hester Prynne—all those interesting, evil, faithless women she had read about in fiction who had never ever

Louise DeSalvo *Adultery*

been Cub Scout den mothers, who had never sat through interminable flute recitals, who had never seen their children portraying roosters in spring pageants.

She would stir the vegetable soup that she was cooking and would contemplate with some deliberation how she would break out of her circle of misery, of meaninglessness, that was, these days, defined by boxes of bean curd and jugs of foul-smelling protein supplement, remembering the veal stews and the chicken soups of her glorious past.

If you were a woman, Helen thought, you turned out to be either a Mrs. Portnoy or a Hester Prynne, and from her current vantage point, she would rather be right up there on the scaffold in the sunlight with Hester than in the kitchen cooking eggplant blintzes or even Portnoy's abused hunk of liver.

Once, soon after she had seen Saturday Night Fever for the fourth time, when the house was quiet and empty, Helen had taken off all her clothes, put on the soundtrack from the film, and had leaped and pirouetted around the family room in imitation of him, watching her breasts flash and her buttocks gleam in the mirror, until she fell onto the sofa, smashing her face into the pillow, laughing in embarrassment, and then crying hot tears for the profligate she had never been.

Actually it wasn't the vegetarianism itself that she minded so much. What she minded so much was the fact that the shelf full of kelp, seaweed, and other vile and nasty bits of detritus from the ocean floor continually reminded her of her girlhood. They reminded her, they reminded her of the things that she would try to avoid in the seawater in those early and idyllic childish days when she had first discovered love, when all the world depended only upon a young man's watery kiss, a young man's hand holding yours, and upon whether or not you could jump higher than the next wave.

Two

The first adultery story I told myself was about my grandfather. In it, he arrives in Italy on board some glamorous steamship that has taken him across the Atlantic Ocean—the *Andrea Doria,* say. This boat trip is far different from the one that brought him to the United States in the first place. Then he traveled because he had to and he came in steerage, carrying a single suitcase. For he was part of the southern Italian diaspora—he left Italy because there was not enough work there to sustain him.

Now, though, he travels because it is his desire that compels him, and his passage is pleasant. Afternoons, he spends sunning himself on deck; evenings, watching the stars that appear in the night sky.

When he arrives, a woman is waiting on the pier to greet him. Unlike my grandmother, she is young, about my mother's age, and she is dazzlingly dressed.

Whatever children he may have sired, though, are not there to meet him. They've been sent to her mother's for the duration of their visit so the two of them can devote the little time they have to enjoying one another.

Before he departs, he will make a ceremonial visit to see the children. They will be beautifully and formally dressed. They will be grateful; they will not cry, whine, nor whimper. They don't mind his continual absence. After all, it is because of him that they have food, they have shelter, they have clothing. For, as she has told them, he takes his responsibilities to them very seriously. They are, after all, his children. Love children. And though she may mind his absences, she never tells him. Perhaps she doesn't mind them. For this relationship they have never bores them. They can go on like this, each admits, for the rest of their lives.

She wears a fitted suit with fur-trimmed collar, a silk blouse, a tissue-thin crimson silk scarf (a present from my grandfather), a hat with a veil, silk stockings, a leather handbag, and sensible but elegant leather pumps. Underneath, she wears panties. They are, of course, made from lace. And they will soon be taken off. She wears no brassiere, no girdle. This woman is voluptuous; she has big breasts, large hips; she doesn't strangle her body with a bra or a corset. She doesn't need to, she doesn't want to.

Louise DeSalvo   *Adultery*

My grandfather loves her ampleness. It welcomes him. It nourishes him. It makes him feel young, virile. She loves her body and the pleasure it gives her (though she has had children, there are no stretch marks); she loves my grandfather's body and the pleasure it gives her.

When she sees him (standing on the railing of the ship, as he always does, which amuses her rather than displeases her as it does my grandmother), she waves a linen handkerchief in welcome. It is hand-embroidered; it has been an early gift from him that she treasures during his long absences (which she never complains about, for she understands that he visits as often as he can).

When he disembarks, they kiss, passionately. Their tongues touch—after all, they haven't seen each other for two or three years. She has hired a horse-drawn carriage to take them home. (Never mind that at this time in Italy even *I* know that lovers zipped through narrow winding city streets on noisy Vespas; he in front, driving; she, in back, clinging. In my adultery story about my grandfather, there is a horse-drawn carriage; it is the nineteenth century.) Inside the carriage, there is a lap robe, two glasses, and a bottle of Asti Spumante, for what else would Italian lovers drink to celebrate their reunion (and what else would a working-class Italian-American teenager in the 1950s *imagine* that Italian lovers would drink)?

But, where is home?

It is, of course, a love nest high on a hill overlooking a body of water; it is reached through narrow winding streets that are lamplit. It has three modest, small, though well-appointed rooms; a balcony where they can linger in the evening before or after their meals or their lovemaking to watch the setting sun reflect its glow on the water. It is on the fifth floor (as love nests often are) and they don't mind the stairs at all. In fact, they run up them (even my grandfather, who seems younger, who even *looks* younger in her presence), unfastening their clothes as they ascend, pausing for soulful kisses on every other landing.

When they are hungry, she doesn't cook; she doesn't have to. In the Italy of my imagination, you need only walk down the stairs, turn right, and, a few doors down, there will be a wonderful purveyor with food and wine for the taking and for next to no money. (This is the only part of the adultery story about my grandfather that turns out to be verifiably true.)

In my adultery story, there is love, there is sex, there is passion, there is food, there is drink, there is pleasure, there is languor. There are naps, there is conversation, there is understanding, there is mutual admiration. There is reading (in bed, in the afternoons, propped up on pink satin pillows). There is even art and music (for they visit museums together, and churches; they attend concerts and operas—my grandfather, I know, could not live very long without opera; in every piazza they traverse, a small group of musicians gathers to serenade the passers-by). There is time enough to satisfy the body, the soul, the mind, and the spirit.

In my adultery story, there is no cooking, no dish-washing, no fights, no one ignoring you (reading the newspaper, looking at television, listening to the radio when you want to share a feeling or an idea). There are no raised voices, no bitterness, no rancor, no sor-row, no leaking toilets or sinks, no lousy landlords, no obnoxious neighbors, no work, no bills, no boring or bad sex, no children present.

Most assuredly, there are no pets. (And so no goldfish bowl to manage; no kitty litter to change; no dogs to walk; no urine stains on the rugs to clean; and no messes deposited by vengeful animals on the kitchen floor or, worse, in the middle of the bed, to scrub.)

In my fantasy of adultery (in everyone's fantasy of adultery) there is no real life. Which, I have come to realize through the years, is precisely what *drives* peo-ple to commit adultery. Because in everybody's fan-tasy of what adultery will be like, there is no real life. (The problems start only when real life intrudes upon adulterous life.) Which is why I imagined that my grandfather went off to Italy to commit adultery. To escape from real life and from responsibility. To become someone other than who he was ordinarily; to become someone other than someone ordinary. To live a life of his own choosing, outside the bounds of law, despite what people thought of him.

In my adultery story, there is romance in abundance. There is desire fulfilled. There is cyclonic sex. There is genuine understanding.

In my adultery story, no one gets caught, no one gets hurt; no marriages dissolve, no families disintegrate. In my adultery story, no woman stands on a pedestal before an assembled crowd, wearing a scarlet *A,* condemned by her townspeople for her misconduct, condemned to a lifetime of isolation because she has chosen to follow the dictates of her own desire. In my adultery story, no one plunges to their death from a church steeple. No woman dies by her own hand. No man shoots his rival.

If my grandfather had such a story as the one I invented for him to tell us, he kept it to himself; he took it to his grave. He was not a lettered man. So, at his death, there was no correspondence (like that of Edith Wharton to W. Morton Fullerton), no journals (like the fictional diaries of Francesca Johnson in Robert James Waller's *The Bridges of Madison County*) that could expose the secrets of a private life. There was nothing that could reveal the clandestine self he might have so scrupulously guarded.

However, my adultery story about my grandfather is not without foundation. As a child, I remember standing on a pier in New York City, wearing my good clothes (pink dress with starched lace collar; natural straw hat; black patent leather shoes and purse; white frilly anklets), and waving a white-gloved hand to my grandfather, who was sailing back to Italy yet again. He stood out from the other passengers because he had climbed onto the ship's railing to wave a large white handkerchief in a grand, sweeping gesture. As the whistles blew and the streamers and confetti fell, I realized that my grandfather, the eternal showman, wasn't so much waving good-bye to his family as he was playing to the crowd.

I always thought that, at moments like these, my grandfather was pretending to be a hero in one of the operas that he adored—*Madame Butterfly, Carmen, La Bohème, La Traviata*. Did he go to Italy so often, I wondered when I was older, to inject the drama of opera into his otherwise humdrum Italian-American working-class life? To see a woman he *really* loved whom he kept there, a *comare?* Or, rather, was it in my fantasies alone that my ordinary barber grandfather became the radiant hero of the operatic stage in an adulterous triangle that existed only in my hyperactive imagination? For it was much more wonderful to be the much beloved granddaughter of a rogue and a rascal than it was to be the much beloved granddaughter of a rather ordinary barber.

And it's true that my grandfather was a shameless exhibitionist and a dandy and that he had very few redeeming qualities. He was brusque, arrogant, argumentative, self-involved. But he was also charismatic and self-assured and extremely self-reliant. Even on ordinary days, my grandfather wore a solid-gold watch chain; carried a hand-hemmed linen handkerchief in his vest pocket; doused himself with expensive cologne. Wouldn't think of leaving the house without his shoes spit-shined. Carried his barber tools in a calfskin pouch. Spent more money on himself than a man in his situation had any right to.

Years later, when I read anthropology, I learn about a breed of man found in many cultures. The "show-off." Jared Diamond, in *Why Is Sex Fun? The Evolution of Human Sexuality* describes him best: among married men, "all of us know some who take better care of themselves than of their wives and children, and who devote inordinate time, money, and energy to philandering and to male status symbols and activities. . . . Much bacon isn't bought home" (102).

This was my grandfather: the "show-off." At one time, this was my husband, too, tooling around in a secondhand but still very flashy and far too expensive red E-Jag convertible while I putter around in an ugly navy-blue Nash Rambler with rotting floorboards. (I still don't understand how I let *that* happen. His driving the Jag; me, the Nash.)

Next to my grandfather, my grandmother looked like a drudge. She spent most of her life in housedresses, covered with neat aprons. Her few good dresses were black (though sometimes there was a frill of lace at the neck). She seemed in perpetual mourning for the happy life that had evaded her, for the husband often not there. While he was away, she earned the money to keep the family, and she always protested his leaving. Still, for his journey, though she wasn't speaking to him, though she often dabbed tears away from her steel gray eyes, she nevertheless pressed his suits, shirts, linen handkerchiefs, and even his underwear, then packed everything carefully, with tissue paper she saved from Christmas to ensure that nothing would wrinkle. For weeks before my grandfather departs, the suitcase lies open on their bedroom floor, a barrier they must cross to get to bed.

What else but my grandfather's having a *comare*, I think, can explain my grandfather's frequent visits to Italy, a country, he tells us often, that he despises? A country that he was lucky to escape from. Years later, reading Helen E. Fisher's *Anatomy of Love: The Natural History of Monogamy, Adultery, and Divorce,*

I learned that, in Italian Adriatic coast towns near where my grandfather was born, "adultery is the rule rather than the exception" and many relationships "last for several years or even life."

Years later, after my grandfather's death, when my own husband is having his first affair, I wonder whether I'm reliving my grandmother's fate (when I so desperately wanted to relive my grandfather's). I wonder whether my husband's behavior might be explained by some kind of cultural imperative dictated by the fact that he, too, is Italian-American. So I ask my father whether my grandfather went back to Italy because of another woman. And he jokingly responds that, though he doesn't know for sure, yes, he has always thought that it was a distinct possibility.

"He was a lulu," my father says. "He left me in charge of the family when I was only seven years old; he left your grandmother without any money to support her and all us kids." My father says this straightforwardly, without as much resentment or rage as I would have liked to hear in his voice, without condemnation. And, it seems, with a tad too much admiration.

Yes, my grandfather was "a lulu," as in "a person who is remarkable," as in "a person who is wonderful." And through the years, this has been my father's nickname for *me*. "Lulu." A nickname that links me with my grandfather.

Which might explain why, all through high school,

I had this habit of dating one boy but sleeping with another. No matter how nice my "official" boyfriend was, no matter how sexy, no matter how smart, no matter how good-looking, no matter how compatible we were, no matter how much necking and petting we did, always, always, I had another boy on the side for fucking. The same boy. A guy named Roy.

To me, my grandfather's trips to Italy, and my stories about them, meant that he refused to let the burden of life diminish him. He seemed a person who, unlike my grandmother, had lived a life without regret. Whatever the cost of his behavior to others, he had fulfilled himself, he had enlarged his life. And I admired him for that, and identified with him, and drew courage from his reprobate spirit.

All I have are unconfirmed suspicions about what my grandfather has done, a story I have told myself about him, and no facts. So he has remained someone I can admire for living a small part of his life precisely as he chose to live it, despite what others thought of him. I honored my grandfather most for refusing to tell whatever story he had to tell. For we never learned why he went back. Perhaps he knew that the private life, the secret life, no matter how innocuous, once it is confessed and once it becomes public, loses its ability to sustain us. A detail in an adultery or an infidelity story only becomes squalid when it's made public. A sordid act is something someone else has done, never something we ourselves have done or imagined ourselves doing.

I start telling myself this adultery story about my grandfather at the end of the ninth grade, beginning of the tenth, about the time that Roy and I begin our erotic relationship in earnest. It's clear, in retrospect, that I am wise beyond my years when it comes to sex, that I have identified with the life I believe my grandfather is living, and that I have begun to see myself as a sexual rebel.

I am a girl not bound by the rules that govern other teenagers, especially other girls. The ones that say you wait for a boy to ask you out; you accept his invitation (whether or not you really want to). You date; you kiss; after a suitable time, you neck, you even pet. But surely you don't fornicate, at least not yet, not when you are fourteen years old. You wait until you're older and until you're sure that he loves you and he's not using you. Or you wait until you're sure you're going to marry him. Or you wait until you marry him.

You certainly don't decide that *he's* the one you want and go after him, even though he's seeing someone else, like I did. You certainly don't proposition him, like I did. And you certainly don't start fucking him in ninth grade, like I did. You don't do any of

these things unless you're a tramp (and I don't see myself as a tramp though others might read my behavior
in this way; how we see ourselves is not necessarily
how others see us) or unless you're liberated.

Me, I think I'm liberated. I'm a freethinker. I've
stopped going to church. I've become an atheist.
An intellectual, though I don't yet feel comfortable
applying the word to myself. I'm reading like crazy
—books that I grab off the shelf of the public library
that help me understand who I am. I'm reading
World War II novels (to find out about my father's
war); Russian novels (to see life lived on a gigantic
scale); biography (to find models for my life); cultural anthropology (to discover the variety of human
behavior); history (to learn about the past). And, of
course, novels about adultery.

One day when I'm in high school, I con my mother
into coming to the library with me to tell the librarian
it's okay for me to read the Kinsey report. It's a volume that's kept locked up; it doesn't circulate; and kids
aren't allowed to read it.

I have told my mother that we're doing a unit on
"Marriage and the Family" for Home Ec., and that
my assignment is to summarize Kinsey. She raises her
eyebrows, which means she doesn't quite believe me,
but she comes with me anyway. She's been coming

to the library for years to tell the librarian it's all right for me to check out books for "adult readers." Once, she admitted that she does it because when I'm reading, she knows where I am and, as she says, "You're out of my hair"—her way of saying I'm not bothering her by asking a million questions or pouting or stirring up trouble.

I have overheard my mother and our next-door neighbor, Dorothy (who has had four children in as many years), talking and laughing about the Kinsey report. (Dorothy laughs raucously; my mother, somewhat uncomfortably.) Dorothy tells my mother that Kinsey says that *everything* people do is normal. Even sex with animals. My mother believes Kinsey says this, but she doesn't think this is true. When I hear them talking, I know I have to read this guy.

"Maybe that's why Tommy brought me home that goddamned dog," Dorothy adds, and starts laughing her throaty smoker's laugh.

Dorothy often seduces my mother into stopping her household "chores," as she refers to them, in the afternoon to relax. Unlike my mother, having floors clean enough to eat from, something my mother prides herself on, is not a high priority for Dorothy. She'd rather share a story, a laugh, and another cup of coffee than wash a floor or scrub a toilet.

I love Dorothy. When I grow up, I want to be just like her. She's the kind of woman who can stir a pot, tend a child, kick the dog away from the defrosting hamburger meat, talk on the telephone, and smoke—all at the same time.

"I don't know how Dotsy does it," my mother always says. "At five o'clock, there's absolutely nothing happening in her kitchen. But by six, when Tommy comes home from work, there's lasagna on the table, piping hot and waiting for him." Cooking well is something my mother has never managed. We're likely to have waffles for dinner or leftover gravy with mashed potatoes or soup meat—stuff I hate, stuff I can't bring myself to eat.

There's so much life in Dorothy's household that it spills into ours through our facing windows. Since she's moved next door, my mother's spirits have lifted. "Dorothy's corrupting you," my father says, grateful.

I'm desperate to read the Kinsey report. I want to find out what "normal" sex is. I also want to find out whether Kinsey says what Dorothy says—that there's no such thing as "kinky" sex. But what I really want to find out is whether what I'm doing with Roy is normal; whether or not *I'm* normal.

And what I discovered when I read Kinsey helps me immeasurably. For I learned that half the women Kinsey studied had sex before they were married. I had started at an age that wasn't all that unusual for working-class girls. And I had a lot to look forward to: premarital "orgasmic experience," as I remember Kinsey putting it, was a good predictor of marital "orgasmic experience."

Rereading Kinsey recently, I realize that as an adolescent, I was like those girls and women he describes whose sexual choices weren't dictated by social mores, but rather by their own consciences. This was the primary way girls and women differed from boys and men, who tended to follow their peers in sexual matters—if their friends were having sex, if their friends or neighbors or colleagues were having extramarital sex, they felt pressured to have it too. For women and girls, though, it was different. They seemed to make their own sexual choices.

In one sense, my affair with Roy was good for me, I learned, when I read Kinsey years ago. For without premarital sexual experience, I found you are far less likely to have a great married sex life. (So much for saving it till you're married, I remembered thinking.) Once a good fuck, always a good fuck. According to Kinsey, I belonged to a select group of sexually responsive females.

Premarital sex was also a good predictor of *extramarital* sexual relationships. And I lingered over the chapter on adultery. What I discovered provided me with a reservoir of information that helped me im-

measurably when my marriage was later tested by
my husband's infidelity. For I read that "interest in a
variety of sexual partners is of ancient standing in
mammalian stocks, and occurs among both females
and males." (These exact words, from my recent
notes.) That many societies permit extramarital activities for the male, less often for the female. But also that
most societies recognize that some restraint on such
behavior is necessary if marriages and homes are to be
maintained.

I understood, too, why people were unfaithful in
marriage: because adultery provided sexual variety;
because it provided social status; because it was an
act of retaliation; because it was an assertion of independence; because it was a source of emotional
satisfaction.

And something I learned served as a warning for
my own behavior, present and future. If a husband
discovers his wife has been unfaithful, the marriage
will far more likely end than if a woman discovers
her husband has been unfaithful. Women and men
don't behave all that differently (although until quite
recently, according to Annette Lawson, more men
had extramarital affairs than women, which is now
not necessarily true). But marriages crumble when
husbands discover what their wives have been doing,
although they don't necessarily disintegrate when

wives discover what their husbands have been doing. (So. If you are a woman, the next time you feel like confessing, unless you want to end your marriage, bear that in mind.)

In those formative years, when I was imagining the kind of marriage I wanted for myself, I had no acceptable models in my family. There was my paternal grandparents' marriage (my grandfather, following his desire; my grandmother, not even believing she had a right to please herself; and a strife-ridden partnership). My maternal grandparents' marriage (a dutiful warring partnership). My parents (a loving union sullied by my mother's depression). But there was the exuberant, fun-filled, raucous, committed relationship of my next-door neighbors, Dorothy and Tommy, who, a half century later, are together still. It broke the mold; it gave me hope. For here were two people who *enjoyed* each other, who laughed together at muddy floors and burned dinners and overdrawn checking accounts, who acted as if living with another person was the most preposterous yet the most miraculous adventure upon which a human being could embark.

What, I wondered, would marriage be like for me? For as unacceptable a state as it sometimes seemed, it never occurred to me not to marry, though I often wondered if it would be possible for me to be monogamous. Infidelity, I sometimes thought, was hardwired into my psyche. Sex on the side, I knew, was risky, powerful, exciting. Sex on the side, I believed, was the best kind of sex to have for it was uncomplicated by the fact of a relationship. Sex on the side, I knew, though, could mess up your life. I had, after all, read *The Scarlet Letter* and *Anna Karenina*. Sex on the side could leave you incapable of doing the things you were supposed to do because you were thinking only of the things you wish you could be doing. Sex on the side could leave you yearning and miserable for weeks on end. Yet sex on the side, I thought, in those days of my young womanhood, was the only kind of sex worth having.

When whatever boyfriend I was currently seeing asked me directly if the rumors he heard were true, if I was sleeping with Roy, I shamelessly looked him straight in the eye and answered, "No, of course I'm not. I wouldn't do that; I wouldn't do that to you." I never said, "It's none of your goddamned business," which is what I wanted to say. I knew, from reading Kinsey, that that would amount to an admission.

For when you're questioned directly about infidelity, about adultery, there is no way to finesse the question that won't indict you and make someone believe you're lying. This is why most people choose a straightforward denial even if, later, it gets them into trouble. (And, as we have seen, in the case of President Clinton, a lot of trouble.) Unless I wanted the relationship to end, I had no choice but to lie about Roy. (And if I needed to now, I would answer as I did then.)

Roy and I meet surreptitiously at his house on Friday nights when he baby-sits his sister; we make love on a sofa overlooking the valley of the town where we live. Or we meet in the small patch of woods behind the brook that runs through our town—the only remnant of a hardwood forest that once covered the valley. We make love on the ground; we use his coat or my coat for a blanket.

This lasts, off and on, until my future husband and I start dating in my junior year of college, when I believe that I will give up the allure of surreptitious, illicit sex forever. Ernie knows, though, about Roy. Once, when we double-dated (Ernie's with a friend of mine; I'm with Roy), Ernie hears me having sex with Roy in an adjoining room. He tells me this, years later, when we're married.

When Ernie and I start dating, he doesn't touch me for weeks; I don't come on to him either. Later he tells me it's because he doesn't want me to think he's just out for "one thing."

It's clear to me that, as a teenager, I identified with the phantom grandfather that I had invented, one

who was as captivating to me, though he was a creature of my own making, as the heroes and heroines
of the operatic plots that also seized my imagination.
I knew I wanted something more from this life I
was leading than the banal and routine life I saw my
parents living—the routine drudgery of work, child-
rearing, and householding. I wanted escape. From
my sorrow. From my home life where my mother and
her stepmother fought incessantly and where both
my mother and my sister were so often depressed
that I called my house "the morgue." There was for
me no soporific as powerful, as cheap, and as available as sex.

I wanted much more for myself than my ordinary
teenage life could provide me. And like so many others
who are dissatisfied with their lives, I believed that the
simplest way to break free from my problems was to
have sex. But not just any sex: surreptitious sex; outlaw sex; extraordinary sex. Without knowing it, I was
replicating a pattern familiar to most grown-ups who
choose adultery.

And, though in some ways this behavior of mine
did set me apart from my peers, and *did* mark me as
a sexual rebel, my story is far more complex than it
seemed, and far more complex than I then knew. For
I had led a hypersexualized life from childhood. Not
only because of my fantasies about my grandfather.
Not only because, as a child, I shared a bedroom with

my parents and witnessed their frequent, vigorous lovemaking and so was as familiar with sex as I was with eating and sleeping.

In a caregiver's home, at a very young age—at five or six or so—I become the object of her overardent attention. I am sent there because my mother is depressed. This I don't realize until I am in my forties, until I'm studying the life of Virginia Woolf, until I understand the parallels between my life and hers as an incest survivor.

I never tell my parents. I never tell my father. Perhaps I know that if I tell my father, there will be violence, there might even be murder, for I have seen how enraged my father can become at me for far less cause.

As I recall (and I don't recall much, at least not directly, for what I remember is fragmented, confused, muddled, as these memories so often are), I wasn't told not to tell. I simply knew I was not to tell. And I knew, too, that I wasn't to remember. At least not with my mind. Though remember, I did, with my body.

Mine was one of those childish bodies that took pleasure against its will. And sometimes not against its will. And I was one of those children who felt immense guilt for the enjoyment I took in what, after all, I hadn't chosen, hadn't wanted to happen. The body often has a mind of its own.

Outlaw sex, surreptitious sex was the sex I learned young. It was, for years, I feared, the only sex that could please me.

What passes for sexual freedom is, I think, often the outgrowth of early abuse. Of early, deep-seated (often unrecognized) loss and sorrow. Of a mourning for innocence lost. Of a grief too deep to bear for the irrevocably damaged child. Sexual distraction is a powerful antidote to pain.

Years later, when I read Alice Munro's *Lives of Girls and Women* for the first time, I find that her teenage character Del is a girl very much like I was as a teenager, but far less troubled.

Del Jordan is the most wholesome and vital young woman I've encountered in fiction; I wish I could have read about her in my teens. As it describes Del's growth, *Lives* renounces several stereotypes about sexual initiation: that we can't establish sound sexual relationships without having emotionally stable adult models; that an early experience with perversity is necessarily ruinous; that sexuality based upon physical attraction alone is unwholesome; that young women should not explore their sexuality as young men do (although all should act responsibly).

Lives of Girls and Women describes Del's sexual initiation with Mr. Chamberlain, an older man, and the excitement and power she feels because she has aroused sexual feelings in him. She expected sex to be vicious and violent because of the literary works she'd read, so she tries to find herself an experience to replicate the ones in books: "a flash of insanity, a dreamlike, ruthless, contemptuous breakthrough in a world of decent appearances." And she finds this with Mr. Chamberlain.

She discovers (as I did) that she likes the feelings in her body, though she knows there is something wrong with Mr. Chamberlain. She doesn't destroy herself with guilt because of what she's done; instead, she learns a valuable lesson: that nowhere but in fantasy do bodies come together "free of thought, free of personality, into self-indulgence." Instead, people "take along a good deal— . . . all the stubborn puzzle and dark turns of themselves" when they take themselves into sex.

In "Baptizing," Del has her first chosen love affair. She falls in love with a boy named Garnet—it is primarily a physical passion; it is "only sex." Del says, "I was surprised, when I thought about it—am surprised still—at the light, even disparaging tone that is taken, as if this was something that could be found easily, every day."

With Garnet, Del has her first shared orgasm in an

encounter that lands them in her mother's peonies. She has had several by herself with "ravenous, imaginary lovers." After her experience with Garnet, Del thinks that orgasm is "almost too private, even lonely a thing, to find at the heart of love."

But when Garnet tries to exert power over her, when he tries to baptize Del into his own brand of Christianity as they swim together, she resists him, and she learns her power: "I felt amazement, not that I was fighting with Garnet but that anybody could have made such a mistake to think he had real power over me." What Del learns through her sexual experience with Garnet is that she will never allow herself to be dominated by a man; never allow herself to be dominated by anyone. Through sex, she has learned about the sanctity of her integrity as a human being. This, too, though far more painfully, is what I learned of myself with Roy.

Years after my affair with Roy, I read the diaries of Anaïs Nin, before the unexpurgated volumes were published. She fascinated me, because I wondered whether her libertine ways—her numerous adulteries, sleeping with her analysts, sleeping with two men on the same day, for example—were freely chosen or rather compelled by something that had happened to her in childhood. I questioned whether they were a sign of her emotional health or of her neurosis. In reading Nin, as in reading *Munro's Lives of Girls and Women*, I was trying to excavate the reasons for my adolescent sexual behavior.

I never identified with Nin. No, never. When reading her, I often felt like throwing the volume through the nearest window in exasperation. Sometimes I thought that if I had been in Nin's presence, I would want to throw *her* through the window. On almost every page, there was a statement that made me want to throw up. "The truth is, I find it impossible to resist the tremendous pleasure of charming, flirting, even when I am not in love. What a confession!" "Only you, my diary, know that it is here I show my fears, weaknesses, my complaints, my disillusions. I feel I cannot be weak outside because others depend on me. I rest my head here and weep."

I couldn't understand this behavior in a woman. I thought, in her own way, that Nin was as sexually enslaved as the narrator in *The Story of O*.

Still, there was something I knew that Nin could teach me. So, I pressed on, and read more than I cared to. And finally found what I looked for in the unexpurgated diaries, and finally found the explanation I had sought in a chapter on Nin in Suzette Henke's *Shattered Subjects*.

Nin, as a child, Henke explains, had had adultery very much on her mind because Joaquin Nin, her father, abandoned the family after a love affair. Nin began her diary after her father's departure as a way of reconnecting with him.

But Nin was physically abused by her father and, according to her testimony, sexually molested by him as well—this, accompanied by beatings. As a grown woman, Nin slept with her father to try to undo his hold over her, as her diary *Incest* recounts. Not surprisingly, the strategy didn't work; it repeated the trauma of her past.

Though my grandfather spent so much time with me, his attentions to me were never transgressive as Nin's father's were to her. That my grandfather was a magnetic presence to me is surely true, and this is why I believe he occupied so much psychic space during my late childhood and young adulthood. That my grandfather could never be mine was true too, for my stories about him were rife with yearning. But thinking about him kept me from thinking about my abusive caregiver.

Nin's father, like my grandfather, often traveled; he was a concert pianist. Unlike my grandfather, Joaquin Nin's never returned to his family.

Early in her life, Nin decided that she didn't want to be like her mother—the betrayed, abandoned, suffering wife. Instead, she wanted to be "like the women who had enchanted and seduced my father, the mistresses who lured him away from us."

In time, as Henke observes, Nin mimicked her

absent father's "fierce sexual independence" together with "his aesthetic sophistication." As Nin herself said, "I *became* my father." But Nin was deluded in her belief that, through her sexual behavior, she manifested her autonomy and control. Instead, she repeated the trauma of her past in her present, while using her work (her half century of journal writing, but also her novels like *House of Incest* and *Winter of Artifice*) to "exorcise" his impact upon her and to prevent her psychic disintegration.

What Nin wrote about her father I could easily have written about my grandfather, though in far more tempered prose. "To me," Nin writes, " 'Father' is a mystery, a vision, a dream. What infinitely beautiful stories I have wound around that magic name. . . . Father! All my life has been one great longing for you."

What I am doing with Roy is counterpoised against the story I tell myself about my grandfather. I need a phantasmagoric ally, it seems, for my own behavior with Roy, for we officially start reading about the perils and pitfalls of adultery and infidelity in our English classes in ninth and tenth grades, when we study Greek mythology.

We learn about Zeus and all those illegitimate children of his. We hear what his continuously enraged wife, Hera, does to this one and that one when she finds

But Ron knows this can't be true. He knows his mother keeps her electric shaver in her bedroom and that she only uses it there. She has lectured him a hundred times about the danger of electricity. The only time she's smacked him as a teenager was when he tried to blow-dry his hair in the bathroom. His father's story, he knows, can't be true. His father, he fears, has killed his mother. And all because of him. All because he told his father about his mother's affair.

Hearing these stories, though, doesn't stop me from carrying on with Roy. Could it be that I want to get caught, that I want to get punished, that I want someone to put a stop to what I'm doing, that I know that what I'm doing is making my life more complicated than it needs to be? Am I addicted to the high that this kind of sex provides?

Through all these years, do I ever think about how Roy's girlfriend must have felt? Not once. She knew, I'm sure. She was betrayed by us both. She forgave him, for I know she stayed with him. Married him. Years later, when I encountered my husband's adultery, I thought back to that early time. I remembered her. She had been my rival and I hated her for no other reason. Now, though, I knew what it felt like to have another woman sleeping with your partner. It didn't feel good.

that Zeus has, yet again, been sleeping around; that he has, yet again, sired another half-god, half-human.

I have little sympathy for Hera because, in my own young life, I am in the position of that other woman whom Hera torments.

Vengeance toward the other woman (murder, for example), I learn, is to be expected from a woman whose man (or god, as the case may be) has been untrue. And, yes, I am the victim of revenge to some small degree. For more than anything in the world, I want to be a cheerleader. I practice back jumps, splits, cartwheels and perform them, so my friends say, as well as anyone else trying out for the cheerleading squad. But because *she* is a cheerleader and, since in our town, cheerleaders *choose* cheerleaders, a cheerleader I will never be.

It could have been worse, I know. It could have been far, far worse. Still, I suffered the rejection, though I know now that not being a cheerleader was a very good thing. Instead of practicing cheerleading, I read; I wrote; I had odd jobs; I saved lots of money.

How much worse Roy's girlfriend's vengeance could have been I learn from my friends' infidelity and adultery stories. They tell them to me, I'm sure, to stop me from doing what I'm doing because they feel sure that my troubles aren't over, that my sleeping with Roy will just have to turn out bad.

My friend Ellen tells me about Renee—some girl

she knows in the town where she grew up who slept with her friend Veronica's boyfriend. When Veronica found out, Susan says, she went nuts. She grabbed a crowbar from her father's garage and went looking for her rival. She found her, parked, in the lot behind the high school, listening to some music and talking with friends.

Veronica takes the crowbar and smashes the window on Renee's side of the car. Everyone in the car starts screaming. Renee tries to start the engine, but it won't turn over. A guy sitting in the back decides he'll jump out of the car, he'll subdue Veronica. But Veronica turns around and holds the crowbar like a baseball bat and hits this guy on the side of the head. He collapses onto the pavement.

By now, Renee has started the car and she's too afraid to see what will happen next, so she drives off. All she wants to do is get away from Veronica. She goes to the police station, tells the cops. What is happening now, whether the guy is all right, Susan doesn't know, but she does know that Veronica is in trouble, Renee is in trouble, and that there will be some kind of trial.

Worse still is another story I hear from my friend Ron. This one is about a guy who feels sure that his mother is fooling around with one of his father's good friends. He's seen them together in this guy's car when he and his friends are cruising up the Palisades Inter-

state Parkway some afternoon when they cut school. None of his friends spot her, but he gets a good look at her when they pass the car. His mother looks happier riding in that car than he's ever seen her.

That night, after his father comes home, at the dinner table, Ron's friend asks his mother what she's been doing that afternoon. She flushes, and says she's spent the day at the library. Ron's friend presses. Asks his mother what she's read, what she's taken home. Her answers don't satisfy.

Ron's friend is pissed and he decides to keep an eye on his mother. And sure enough, he spots her again with his father's friend. Now he's sure, so he tells his father. His father doesn't say much. He thanks his son; he tells him not to tell anybody.

Months pass and not much happens. Ron's friend's parents seem civil enough to one another, though the household atmosphere is tense. It's clear from the circles under his mother's eyes that she's been losing sleep. Ron's friend feels sure that the romance is over and he thinks, in time, everything will be normal.

During the summer, though, when Ron's friend is away at camp, his father calls to tell him that his mother has died. It has been an accident. Ron's friend's mother has stupidly decided to use an electric shaver while she was taking a bath; the appliance has fallen into the tub; his mother has been electrocuted. Fortunately, she didn't suffer; her death was instantaneous

In the eleventh grade, in American Literature, we read *The Scarlet Letter* in our English class. As I recall, though we spend much time reading this work, and discussing it, the teacher never once mentions sex and never once defines adultery. Still, *I* know what all that fuss is about in Salem. But I have a different take on the book from my teacher and from most of the kids in my class.

For one thing, I know the novel is a fraud, and I say so. The teacher ignores my remark.

I have been reading Puritan history for background, and I know that the punishment for adultery in Puritan New England isn't wearing a nicely embroidered *A* on your bosom, enduring the censuring stares of townspeople, and then voluntarily and rather defiantly sticking around the community while you raise your child and eventually become an angel of mercy. No.

I know that the least severe punishment for adultery was one or two severe public whippings, potentially life-threatening because of the possibility of subsequent infection. Women convicted of the lesser crime of fornication were whipped and had their children taken from them; women convicted of adultery could easily share this fate. So I knew that Nathaniel Hawthorne's book presented the destiny of an adulteress as far less severe than the historical record showed.

(Years later, when I write a book about Hawthorne, I think I discover why. Hawthorne's Puritan forebears who spelled their name *Hathorne* were especially tyrannical magistrates. One was so despotic that his jurisdiction over the punishment of Quakers was removed from him by Charles II. Hawthorne's ancestors routinely meted out severe punishments. One forebear ordered the children of Quakers into slavery and starved the Quakers themselves to death. Another ordered the boring of holes through women's tongues with red-hot irons, the cutting off of men's ears. Another was responsible for the hanging of five women as witches.

Hawthorne, I now believe, misrepresented history to exculpate consciously or unconsciously the members of his family. They surely would have treated a Hester Prynne far more severely than Hawthorne's historically inaccurate portrayal.)

Some years ago, I happened upon my high school copy of *The Scarlet Letter*. Leafing through it, I read its underlinings and marginal notes—most, it seems, dictated by the teacher. "Chillingworth is guilty of the sin of trying to dominate another human being." "Dimmesdale should have confessed his deed so that he, like Hester Prynne, could have been joined to the rest of humanity through publicly proclaiming his guilt."

But one comment stood out, revealing the rebel I was even then. Next to a description of Hester's ennoblement through suffering, I had written in red pen, underlined and with three adolescent exclamation points, the single word, *"Fool!!!"* For I didn't think it was good for Hester not to have spoken openly about her relationship with Dimmesdale—I believed it was needlessly self-sacrificing for her to bear her suffering alone. But neither did I think it was evil of Dimmesdale to hide his "sin"—I thought that private sexual behavior should remain private.

Studying the novel angered and perplexed me, for I railed at the talk about who should or should not have been punished for their sins; about whether or not their sins should have been openly admitted so punishment could be properly meted out. I wanted to discuss whether what Hester did could properly be called a "sin" at all, even according to Puritan standards; I wanted to discuss why women were thought to be fundamentally base in Puritan culture; I wanted a frank discussion of the horrific punishments of the Puritans, and of when adultery or infidelity was permissible, and if so under what conditions. We never had these discussions, of course. Sober discourse about adultery, Kinsey understood, was difficult if not impossible.

Why, I wondered, were we reading this book anyway? Were we reading it to warn us away from sex? To teach us that if we behaved like Hester we might find ourselves with a little Pearl to raise all by ourselves? To teach us that if we were unfaithful, our culture would exact its punishment from us? To warn us away from adultery when we married?

It would take more than reading *The Scarlet Letter*, though, to stop me. Often Roy and I would joke about how, after we had each married other people (for we felt sure we would marry other people), we'd sleep together anyway. We wouldn't let a little thing like marriage stand in the way of our passion.

It never occurred to me that Roy and I would marry. He had his girlfriend; I had my boyfriends. And I didn't want to spoil our sex by making our relationship public. But for years I believed that one of the major reasons I would marry was so that one day I could commit adultery with Roy.

When I was involved with Roy, of course, I wrote poems. A sheaf of them. Penned at the desk my father had built me at the top of the second-floor landing when I was supposed to be doing physics or geometry homework. Carefully filed, according to date, in an innocuous folder marked "Fragments" that I kept in my desk drawer and that my mother probably read when she rifled through it searching, I suppose, for proof that I was doing what I was in fact doing.

Years later, after I was married, I gathered them

that Zeus has, yet again, been sleeping around; that he has, yet again, sired another half-god, half-human.

I have little sympathy for Hera because, in my own young life, I am in the position of that other woman whom Hera torments.

Vengeance toward the other woman (murder, for example), I learn, is to be expected from a woman whose man (or god, as the case may be) has been untrue. And, yes, I am the victim of revenge to some small degree. For more than anything in the world, I want to be a cheerleader. I practice back jumps, splits, cartwheels and perform them, so my friends say, as well as anyone else trying out for the cheerleading squad. But because *she* is a cheerleader and, since in our town, cheerleaders *choose* cheerleaders, a cheerleader I will never be.

It could have been worse, I know. It could have been far, far worse. Still, I suffered the rejection, though I know now that not being a cheerleader was a very good thing. Instead of practicing cheerleading, I read; I wrote; I had odd jobs; I saved lots of money.

How much worse Roy's girlfriend's vengeance could have been I learn from my friends' infidelity and adultery stories. They tell them to me, I'm sure, to stop me from doing what I'm doing because they feel sure that my troubles aren't over, that my sleeping with Roy will just have to turn out bad.

My friend Ellen tells me about Renee—some girl

she knows in the town where she grew up who slept with her friend Veronica's boyfriend. When Veronica found out, Susan says, she went nuts. She grabbed a crowbar from her father's garage and went looking for her rival. She found her, parked, in the lot behind the high school, listening to some music and talking with friends.

Veronica takes the crowbar and smashes the window on Renee's side of the car. Everyone in the car starts screaming. Renee tries to start the engine, but it won't turn over. A guy sitting in the back decides he'll jump out of the car, he'll subdue Veronica. But Veronica turns around and holds the crowbar like a baseball bat and hits this guy on the side of the head. He collapses onto the pavement.

By now, Renee has started the car and she's too afraid to see what will happen next, so she drives off. All she wants to do is get away from Veronica. She goes to the police station, tells the cops. What is happening now, whether the guy is all right, Susan doesn't know, but she does know that Veronica is in trouble, Renee is in trouble, and that there will be some kind of trial.

Worse still is another story I hear from my friend Ron. This one is about a guy who feels sure that his mother is fooling around with one of his father's good friends. He's seen them together in this guy's car when he and his friends are cruising up the Palisades Interstate Parkway some afternoon when they cut school. None of his friends spot her, but he gets a good look at her when they pass the car. His mother looks happier riding in that car than he's ever seen her.

That night, after his father comes home, at the dinner table, Ron's friend asks his mother what she's been doing that afternoon. She flushes, and says she's spent the day at the library. Ron's friend presses. Asks his mother what she's read, what she's taken home. Her answers don't satisfy.

Ron's friend is pissed and he decides to keep an eye on his mother. And sure enough, he spots her again with his father's friend. Now he's sure, so he tells his father. His father doesn't say much. He thanks his son; he tells him not to tell anybody.

Months pass and not much happens. Ron's friend's parents seem civil enough to one another, though the household atmosphere is tense. It's clear from the circles under his mother's eyes that she's been losing sleep. Ron's friend feels sure that the romance is over and he thinks, in time, everything will be normal.

During the summer, though, when Ron's friend is away at camp, his father calls to tell him that his mother has died. It has been an accident. Ron's friend's mother has stupidly decided to use an electric shaver while she was taking a bath; the appliance has fallen into the tub; his mother has been electrocuted. Fortunately, she didn't suffer; her death was instantaneous.

But Ron knows this can't be true. He knows his mother keeps her electric shaver in her bedroom and that she only uses it there. She has lectured him a hundred times about the danger of electricity. The only time she's smacked him as a teenager was when he tried to blow-dry his hair in the bathroom. His father's story, he knows, can't be true. His father, he fears, has killed his mother. And all because of him. All because he told his father about his mother's affair.

Hearing these stories, though, doesn't stop me from carrying on with Roy. Could it be that I want to get caught, that I want to get punished, that I want someone to put a stop to what I'm doing, that I know that what I'm doing is making my life more complicated than it needs to be? Am I addicted to the high that this kind of sex provides?

Through all these years, do I ever think about how Roy's girlfriend must have felt? Not once. She knew, I'm sure. She was betrayed by us both. She forgave him, for I know she stayed with him. Married him. Years later, when I encountered my husband's adultery, I thought back to that early time. I remembered her. She had been my rival and I hated her for no other reason. Now, though, I knew what it felt like to have another woman sleeping with your partner. It didn't feel good.

In the eleventh grade, in American Literature, we read *The Scarlet Letter* in our English class. As I recall, though we spend much time reading this work, and discussing it, the teacher never once mentions sex and never once defines adultery. Still, *I* know what all that fuss is about in Salem. But I have a different take on the book from my teacher and from most of the kids in my class.

For one thing, I know the novel is a fraud, and I say so. The teacher ignores my remark.

I have been reading Puritan history for background, and I know that the punishment for adultery in Puritan New England isn't wearing a nicely embroidered *A* on your bosom, enduring the censuring stares of townspeople, and then voluntarily and rather defiantly sticking around the community while you raise your child and eventually become an angel of mercy. No.

I know that the least severe punishment for adultery was one or two severe public whippings, potentially life-threatening because of the possibility of subsequent infection. Women convicted of the lesser crime of fornication were whipped and had their children taken from them; women convicted of adultery could easily share this fate. So I knew that Nathaniel Hawthorne's book presented the destiny of an adulteress as far less severe than the historical record showed.

(Years later, when I write a book about Hawthorne, I think I discover why. Hawthorne's Puritan forebears who spelled their name *Hathorne* were especially tyrannical magistrates. One was so despotic that his jurisdiction over the punishment of Quakers was removed from him by Charles II. Hawthorne's ancestors routinely meted out severe punishments. One forebear ordered the children of Quakers into slavery and starved the Quakers themselves to death. Another ordered the boring of holes through women's tongues with red-hot irons, the cutting off of men's ears. Another was responsible for the hanging of five women as witches.

Hawthorne, I now believe, misrepresented history to exculpate consciously or unconsciously the members of his family. They surely would have treated a Hester Prynne far more severely than Hawthorne's historically inaccurate portrayal.)

Some years ago, I happened upon my high school copy of *The Scarlet Letter.* Leafing through it, I read its underlinings and marginal notes—most, it seems, dictated by the teacher. "Chillingworth is guilty of the sin of trying to dominate another human being." "Dimmesdale should have confessed his deed so that he, like Hester Prynne, could have been joined to the rest of humanity through publicly proclaiming his guilt."

But one comment stood out, revealing the rebel I was even then. Next to a description of Hester's ennoblement through suffering, I had written in red pen, underlined and with three adolescent exclamation points, the single word, *"Fool!!!"* For I didn't think it was good for Hester not to have spoken openly about her relationship with Dimmesdale—I believed it was needlessly self-sacrificing for her to bear her suffering alone. But neither did I think it was evil of Dimmesdale to hide his "sin"—I thought that private sexual behavior should remain private.

Studying the novel angered and perplexed me, for I railed at the talk about who should or should not have been punished for their sins; about whether or not their sins should have been openly admitted so punishment could be properly meted out. I wanted to discuss whether what Hester did could properly be called a "sin" at all, even according to Puritan standards; I wanted to discuss why women were thought to be fundamentally base in Puritan culture; I wanted a frank discussion of the horrific punishments of the Puritans, and of when adultery or infidelity was permissible, and if so under what conditions. We never had these discussions, of course. Sober discourse about adultery, Kinsey understood, was difficult if not impossible.

Why, I wondered, were we reading this book anyway? Were we reading it to warn us away from

sex? To teach us that if we behaved like Hester we might find ourselves with a little Pearl to raise all by ourselves? To teach us that if we were unfaithful, our culture would exact its punishment from us? To warn us away from adultery when we married?

It would take more than reading *The Scarlet Letter*, though, to stop me. Often Roy and I would joke about how, after we had each married other people (for we felt sure we would marry other people), we'd sleep together anyway. We wouldn't let a little thing like marriage stand in the way of our passion.

It never occurred to me that Roy and I would marry. He had his girlfriend; I had my boyfriends. And I didn't want to spoil our sex by making our relationship public. But for years I believed that one of the major reasons I would marry was so that one day I could commit adultery with Roy.

When I was involved with Roy, of course, I wrote poems. A sheaf of them. Penned at the desk my father had built me at the top of the second-floor landing when I was supposed to be doing physics or geometry homework. Carefully filed, according to date, in an innocuous folder marked "Fragments" that I kept in my desk drawer and that my mother probably read when she rifled through it searching, I suppose, for proof that I was doing what I was in fact doing.

Years later, after I was married, I gathered them

together, made little piles of them, and finally assembled them into a manuscript that I called, for want of a better title, *Kinds of Love*. I thought I might do something with them. Revise them. Submit them for publication. But time passed and I started to write about other people's lives and other people's loves.

When I turn forty-five, I realize that, if they are found after my death, they will not sound like poems I've written in my teens, but, instead, like poems I've written as a grown woman, as an adulteress. There is so much pain and longing in them, but also, so much ecstasy, that they will surely signify that I was once involved in an illicit affair.

And so, on an icy winter day when my marriage and my children mean very much to me, and fearing that these poems will be found among my papers, and not wanting to cause my family pain, I spend part of a (tearful, of course) afternoon when I am alone rereading them. I tear the manuscript into tiny little pieces and throw them into my wastebasket without regret.

(But not before I memorize a few. Like this one, which I called "La Mer": *I would like to make love to you just once with our bodies all salty from seawater so that we could begin by licking the crystals from one another. You could go first because I can never wait. And then it would be my turn. And we would taste each other slowly pulsating to the rhythm of the sea as it surged outside.*

And this one, which I called "Left Ventricular Fibrillation": *Today I understood for the first time that the heart has parts and that while one part of the heart has experienced a rent a fissure that will widen or heal itself depending upon whether or not you come back to me the other part of the heart can go on doing the things that hearts do most of the time like pump blood from here to there although I cannot imagine why the heart should want to continue doing those things at this particular time.)*

That evening, when Ernie is collecting the trash, he takes the wastepaper basket out from under my desk, brings it into the kitchen, and empties it, in a flurry, onto the remnants of our evening meal.

"Are you okay?" he asks. "It looks like you've had a bad day," he says, cinching the garbage bag shut. In fact, I had had a very good writing day.

"All that paper. All that garbage," he continues. "Looks like you couldn't figure anything out."

"You're right," I lie. "Today was tough. But tomorrow"—I kiss him on the cheek for taking out the garbage and for caring about my work—"might be better."

Three

Just recently, I am sitting at the breakfast table with my husband and he asks me how my work is going. He knows I'm writing a book about adultery, but he thinks I'm writing about important *novels* about adultery— *Anna Karenina, The Scarlet Letter, Madame Bovary.* At least that's what I've told him. He's seen me reading them, underlining them, taking notes on them.

I tell him I'm having a hard time. That though I've done some writing on those works, I'm also writing about us.

"Oh brother," he says. "Do you have to write about it again?" I don't respond. A few minutes later he says, "Of course you have to write about it. I understand."

I must admit that years ago I gloated when one version I wrote about what my husband had done was reported by Carolyn Heilbrun in *Ms.* as an example

of an honest view of the perils of marriage. She paraphrased it from an account I had written in 1983 or thereabouts that was published in a collection of essays called *Between Women*.

My husband's mother picked up the magazine and read it while she was having her hair done at her local beauty parlor and she was horrified. She called my husband at work to tell him what she'd read, and he called me at work to tell me about her call.

And what did I think when I saw it after I heard the despair in my husband's voice? *Serves you right, you bastard,* is what I thought.

Now, I tell my husband I'm writing a chapter that I am referring to as "Anatomy of an Adultery" and that I realize that, to write it, I'll have to find out why he was unfaithful. It's not something we've ever talked about partly because I'm not sure people ever know why they do things like this. So I ask him.

He says he won't answer that question. That, at this stage of our marriage, discussing what happened then won't do us any good now. But he offers, "I really don't know why it happened; I can't say why. I only know that it had nothing to do with you, that it never had anything to do with you, that I never stopped loving you."

I tell him I wished I'd had known that back then, those many years ago. He shrugs.

To begin a telling of my (our) adultery story.
Ernie and I had been married for just over four years.
We married his first semester of medical school,
my first semester of high school teaching. We had
our first baby four years after we married. He was
an intern; I had given up my job teaching high
school English to raise our child, though I intended
to return at some future time. It wasn't something
I chose to do, really; it was what I and almost all the
women I knew did at that time—this, after all, was
the sixties.

I knew I was in trouble when he forgot the time
he was supposed to pick me and the baby up from the
hospital and he arrived very late and very disheveled.
Under ordinary circumstances, he was, like my grandfather, the neatest, the most gorgeously dressed of
men. He was extremely vague about where he had been
and why he had forgotten. Something about a party
some people had given for him for becoming a father.

The excuse sounded phony to me. But I said
nothing. I was too exhausted.

The baby was dressed adorably in standard baby
take-home fare: blue booties, blue cap, little white
stretch suit, hand-knitted (by me) sweater, receiving
blanket. I looked like hell and wore the same soiled
maternity dress I'd worn to the hospital, though I'd
tried to decorate my face for the occasion. On the ride
home (it was snowing out, I remember, somewhat

unusual for November), I knew I had some rough times ahead and not just because of the baby.

Ernie and I had known each other since high school though we hadn't liked each other at all during those years. We had started dating in college. My mother insisted that I start looking for a husband, a man who was what she called a "good catch." I know she knew about Roy—she had overheard more than one of our overheated telephone conversations. She wanted me to put an end to that "episode," as she called it.

If I married well, she said—someone with prospects, someone with a profession, someone who could support me well—all the family's sacrifices will have been worthwhile. I told her that I didn't want to be taken care of by a man, that I could take care of myself, and support myself, and that's why I was going to college. I say that what I want (what I have always wanted) is an equal partner. A man who wants the same things for me that I want for myself. Independence. Freedom. Someone who won't ask me too many questions about what I do. Someone who supports what I want to do whatever that may be.

My mother tells me this isn't what marriage is all about. Marriage is about making sacrifices. My mother says she doesn't think it's possible to find a man like this. But I think I've found this man in Ernie.

Ernie and I get along. When we first reconnect

(over a game of bridge at a mutual friend's house
in the summer of my sophomore year in college,
when I'm still seeing Roy, though I stop, soon after),
he doesn't try to sleep with me. He knows about
my reputation. Once, in fact, he's been in the next
room when Roy and I are having sex. He's afraid
that if he tries to sleep with me, I'll think that all he
wants is sex.

He likes me right away, he says. The way I play
bridge. My wise-ass comments. My brains. My independence. My sweetness. My Italian good looks.
When we start dating, his mother is ecstatic because
he's never dated anyone she's considered suitable.
She thinks I'm suitable. "Don't screw this one up,"
she warns her son. "If you hurt her," she says,
"I'll kill you."

For the first month we date, Ernie and I talk. About
philosophy. Existentialism. Sartre. Camus. Psychol-
ogy. Religion. We play some more bridge. We go to see
foreign films. I like Ernie. We get along, though we
argue a lot. About everything. Politics. Religion. You
name it. But I feel comfortable with him. He's Italian.
He likes pizza. He's sexy. Spent much of his life in an
Italian working-class neighborhood like mine in
Hoboken.

We talk about our future: he's going to be a doctor;
I'm going to be a high school teacher, though some
day, I want to teach college, maybe even write books.

We both want to travel; have children; live a good life (though we don't know exactly what that means but we do know that it means living a balanced life, and not a life consumed by work).

Over the next two years, our lives intertwine. I read Ernie's college papers, he reads mine. He helps me when I get crazy about writing papers, calms me down. We go to the opera together. His favorite is *La Bohème*. He tells me he sings his favorite arias out loud in his car after he drops me off at college. He stops a few miles up the turnpike to call me and tell me that he misses me already.

We talk about marriage and children. He wants to raise them Catholic; I tell him he can do that himself, I'm an atheist. We fight about that; we almost break up. He realizes he's being a hypocrite because he's not a practicing Catholic either, so it will be okay if our children choose their own religion when they're older.

Oh, yes. And we have sex. Good sex, then great sex. Often.

Ernie had wanted to wait until after his graduation from medical school for us to marry. I pushed the marriage because I wanted to move out of my parents' house, and I wanted an independent life, and the only way then for a young woman of my class and background to move out of the family home was to get married.

After Ernie and I marry, we set up our first apartment in Jersey City, New Jersey, close to his medical school, in a safe-enough apartment. We furnish our home with brand-new Danish-modern furniture bought with money we'd saved. For upstairs neighbors, we have hookers who rattle up and down the stairs next to our bedroom all night long. For next-door neighbors, a couple who have screaming fights about his infidelities. The building has a crazy superintendent (who, we think, robs us), and one murder in the four years we lived there before moving to Cranford, New Jersey.

We don't have children for four years because we want to enjoy one another and to travel. We live frugally, on a strict budget, and save every penny we can for travel, our passion. Our only splurges are dinner out one night a week (at a cheap restaurant where he has fried chicken and I have eggplant Parmesan; dinner parties (which we give one night a month—I cook out of a paperback international cookbook); one movie night a week. We spend fifteen dollars a week on food; have five dollars each for spending money. Whatever is left over, we save for travel.

We spend seven weeks in Europe the summer after we marry and four weeks driving cross-country a year later. When we travel, Ernie and I enjoy ourselves most. We like doing the same things. We love taking self-directed walking tours through cities; we love finding the homes of famous writers. We love driving through the countryside; we like small charming cheap hotels, not big lavish ones (which we couldn't afford anyway). We don't like to shop; we are passionate about food (and we cart home treasures like olive oil and herbs); we love having picnics.

Our first four years of marriage are hard, yet exhilarating. I love teaching, though teaching five classes a day, cooking dinner, and keeping the apartment exhausts me. Ernie does well in medical school. He shares housekeeping with me; loves shopping for food, which I hate, though I love to cook.

I love being married and try to be a "good wife"—keeping a neat, well-run home, making nice meals, entertaining well, being a good companion, a good sex partner.

When our son is six months old, Ernie tells me his adultery story. His affair is your basic doctor-in-training-meets-gorgeous-nurse-and-wants-to-leave-his-wife-and-small-baby story. He can't keep it to himself, for whatever reason. Doesn't want to keep it to himself. It isn't that we are among those fools who, in the sixties and seventies, revered honesty above all things, whatever the cost to the self and to the marriage, and he told me because we had promised each other we'd keep no secrets from each other.

Like so many other people, we had never talked

about adultery, fidelity. Frankly, when I thought about the subject, I assumed that if either of us strayed, *I'd* be the one. Unlike me, Ernie had only dated one girl at a time. Never cheated on his girlfriends as I cheated on my boyfriends.

At the time, I thought Ernie wanted out of the marriage and that he wanted me to acquiesce to his breaking our union. For I remember him telling me that he was having an affair with a nurse and that he was thinking of leaving me (us).

When I tell Ernie more about what I'm now writing, he tells me that, though, for years, I have been representing his affair as your basic-doctor-in-training-meets-gorgeous-nurse-and-wants-to-leave-his-wife-and-small-baby story, and though he's never before said anything to dispute me, it wasn't that way at all. In this retelling, he says I should make it clear that she wasn't a nurse and she wasn't gorgeous. And though, at the time, he may have said he was considering it, he really never thought of leaving me.

I tell him that this is *my* story about what happened to us, not his, and that I'll represent it the way I lived it, the way it happened, the way I remember it, and the way I want to. (To me, they're all the same.) I say if *he* wants, one day, he can write *his own* version of the story. This, I'm sure (or hope), he'll never do.

"One writer in the family," my husband often says,

"is enough." In the case of writing about adultery, one writer in the family, I think he thinks, is one more than enough. Especially when the writer is writing about him. One story about this time in our lives, even though it's not quite the right story, is sufficient. And so my story (stories) represents what happened to us, though it might not be what happened to us at all.

I look for models for what I am writing and don't find many. There are, after all, not that many adultery memoirs floating around considering how many people have affairs, considering how many novels are devoted to the subject. Fiction, I realize, is the way many writers, like D. H. Lawrence, tell their adultery stories. Fiction is safer; fiction disguises the fact that you might be writing about yourself.

No, I find that there aren't many evenhanded discussions of adultery in memoir form. Nancy Mairs is one writer I've found who is willing to discuss her affairs though she is still married. And Gay Talese talked about his in *Thy Neighbor's Wife* (though in that book, his affairs are described as necessary "research" for the writing of his book. There are Richard Brzeczek's *Addicted to Adultery;* Inette Miller's *Burning Bridges: Diary of a Mid-Life Affair;* Caroline Buchanan's *Caught in the Act;* H. S. Vigeveno's *I'm in Love with a Married Man;* Lawrence E. Edwards's

Lover: The Confessions of a One-Night Stand; Robert
Travers's *The Amorous Dentist: A True Story* (which,
I confess, I'd love to read if only I could get my hands
on it; I've been trying). And soon we'll have *Monica's
Story.* Maybe even Linda Tripp's story. (Will we ever
have Bill's?)

When Alfred S. Kinsey was writing about the effects
of adultery, he reported that not many accounts existed
about adulteries that *did not* end marriages. It was extremely difficult, he said, to get honest answers from
people about their adulterous experiences or the effect
of adultery on their lives even when he promised
absolute confidentiality. He speculated that there is
something so shameful, so potentially dangerous about
having adultery made public, that most people choose
to keep silent, or, when confronted, to lie about it.

So a work like the literary critic John Bayley's *Elegy
for Iris,* which speaks forthrightly about the place of
adultery in his forty-year-long marriage to the novelist and philosopher Iris Murdoch is unusual, as what
I am trying to do here is unusual. I love what Bayley
has to say about his acceptance of Murdoch's rejection
of a monogamous union. Murdoch rejected the stric-
ture of fidelity within marriage because she saw it as
curtailing her freedom. She desired, though, much of
what marriage offers—companionship, comfort, a
sense of safety. Her view of marriage, Bayley believes,

was as protean as she was; she saw no reason why she couldn't remake the institution to suit her needs.

Part of the fabric of their marriage was Murdoch's insistence on her right to privacy and to having a separate life, which included love affairs. She told Bayley that they did not reflect upon their relationship or her love for him. He was jealous, of course. But he says this:

> In the early days, I always thought it would be vulgar—as well as not my place—to give any indications of jealousy, but she knew when it was there, and she soothed it just by being the self she always was with me, which I soon knew to be wholly and entirely different from any way that she was with other people.

Here, then, is a marriage that coexisted quite nicely with adultery. It was a marriage Mary Gordon describes in the *New York Times Book Review* as "a marriage of domestic closeness, of shared routines, shared jokes, rituals, songs, of physical proximity and the dependability of seeing each other regularly."

My favorite adultery memoir, though, is Colette's *My Apprenticeships*. It talks, frankly, about how unhealthy and unwholesome living in an adulterous household can be. "Would you have stayed with your husband," I was once asked, after I had published the essay about our life together, "if you had known he would continue to have affairs?" "Most certainly not," I answered. "It would have killed me." But then I quickly appended, "Unless he kept them quiet; unless they didn't interfere with my life or that of our children," knowing this was an impossibility, knowing that living a secret life contaminates the air in a household as imperceptibly but as lethally as radon.

Colette writes what happened to her. How living with adultery "taught me my most essential art, which is not that of writing, but the domestic art of knowing how to wait, to conceal, to save up crumbs, to reglue, regild, change the worst into the not-so-bad." But also, "how to lose and recover in the same moment that frivolous thing, a taste for life."

She speaks of how her husband Willy's adulteries literally made her sick. Of how his spending money on other women meant that she went without a warm coat in the winter. Of how she felt like a prisoner within her marriage. Of how she lost her soul. Of how she started, nonetheless, to write. She wrote of how an important friendship saved her, how it restored her eroded confidence, and nourished her betrayed spirit. And of how she struggled out, unaided, from her marriage, "from the mass of bricks, mortar, planks and plaster that had fallen" on her head.

Colette writes of how adultery becomes a succubus.

Of how the most prevalent feeling she had in her marriage was one of dread, of waiting for the other shoe to fall.

Dread, the constant companion, Colette observes, of the cheated-upon spouse. Dread, the feeling that contaminates the most hopeful soul, that turns the world into a terrifying place.

In the years since Ernie's adultery, long after I believe I have put this episode behind me, I repeatedly have the following nightmare.

I dream about a gigantic cliff somewhat like Beachy Head in Sussex, England, where I have journeyed more than once with Ernie and our sons. In my dream, the cliffside is fitted with a fast-moving escalator that takes passengers from the seaside up onto the summit.

On this day, the only people riding the escalator are women with the impassive features of the women in Paul Delvaux's *Village of the Mermaids* who carry babies in their arms, and me. Each woman stares wide-eyed at nothing in particular; each has well-formed breasts bulging slightly beneath the long gray ascetic garment she wears; each seems to be resigned to whatsoever awaits her at the top.

I, though, am terribly agitated and try to warn the others to be on their guard, but no one heeds me. At the top of the escalator, you must throw this baby you've been carrying back down onto the rocky ground below and jump down the cliffside yourself in time to catch the baby. This, of course, is nearly impossible.

A few women are successful, as I am, and they hold their babies tight after they catch them. But many others aren't, and their babies die as they smash to the ground.

The women, heedless of what has happened, walk over to the base of the escalator to pick up yet another baby (from a conveyor-belt-type contraption) at the base of the cliff to begin the journey again.

There are no men in this dream. Only impassive women. Only dying babies. Only a few women capable as I am of mastering this horrific, endless task.

As *I* jump, it seems that I too won't reach the ground in time to catch my baby. But I do. I always do.

If my husband had *his* way, I think he wishes I wouldn't have written about our life, wouldn't be writing about it now, that I wouldn't be adding my name to those few people who've "come out" as, what— adultery survivors? Am I an adultery survivor? Is surviving adultery something like surviving other forms of abuse? Am I writing my own guide to surviving adultery even though there are a few adultery survival guides, all written for women?

But my husband never tries to stop me from writing this. I would consider his trying to stop me from writing my adultery story even more of a violation than having an adultery story to tell. For *that* would be a violation of my autonomy, whereas his committing adultery, or however you choose to phrase it, is not.

As he admits, he had it coming to him—my writing about him, that is. And, as he may not admit, there are worse things than being cast in the role of a sexual libertine whose marriage did not fall apart. Considering what he put me (us) through, he says, I didn't repay him as savagely as I could have.

And, yes, in case you're interested, I've forgiven him, if I am entitled to forgiveness here. But surely I have not forgotten. His affair, and my memory of it, and my reconstruction of it, after all, have served me well. They have taught me much. I am who I am because of it. I cannot imagine who I would have been without it. Among the things I have become is a realist, which, for a woman, is certainly better than being an incurable romantic who believes that marriage to the right man will inevitably bring a lifetime of happiness.

I have become a person who believes in Virginia Woolf's definition of marriage as "solitude without loneliness," which might not strike some (those who believe in communion and commingling in marriage) as sheer bliss. Among the things I have also become because of Ernie's adultery is even more fiercely independent than I had been, which, for a woman, is certainly not a bad idea.

I think by saying that I haven't repaid him as I might have my husband means to say that I have never had a retaliatory affair. Or that I have never told him about an affair that I *did* have. Perhaps my husband assumes that if I had had an affair, I would have told him about it the way he told me. (I wouldn't.) Perhaps he assumes that his way of handling infidelity would be mine also. (It wouldn't.)

Actually, he has never asked me for this information. "You can't ever keep a secret," he tells me often, more, I think, to reassure himself that I *don't* have a secret life than to comment upon what he knows to be true about me. Because at other times he also says, "You would have made a great spy," when he remarks on my ability to keep silent. He's right: I could have been. And I have. Kept secrets, that is. Mine. And other people's.

I'm not one of those people you tell something to, tell them not to tell anybody, but knowing that what you told them will be spread all around. (This happens, I know, in politics.) If you tell me not to tell, I won't. Of that you can be sure. Perhaps because of this, I have become the repository of more adultery stories than I would like. Stories I can't share here.

I think my husband thinks he knows me very well and so, because he knows some things about me, he knows all things about me. And, in some ways, he does know me. He knows that I prefer eating at home to eating in restaurants; that I view a bad meal as a near tragedy; that I prefer Italy to France; that I prefer Sag Harbor to any other place in the world; that I will only knit with wool, silk, or cotton; that I must see my sons and daughter-in-law and grandson weekly and hear from them every few days—I am, after all, Italian-American, that I love presents but that I don't like surprises; that I love to bake bread, knit complex sweaters, and read books more than I like to socialize; that I detest television but that I love movies.

But what I think my husband does not know is that people who live together are always in many ways perfect strangers to each other. For, as Sally Seton says in Virginia Woolf's *Mrs. Dalloway*, "for what can one know even of the people one lives with every day?" Because we know how the other person brushes their teeth, and makes love, and balances (or, as in my husband's case, *does not* balance) their checkbooks, and the (often absurd or adorable) routines they need to start their day, and that they do or do not like heights or the seaside or pizza or mystery novels or traveling or television or black-and-white movies, we assume that we *know* them, which of course we don't.

And thinking about the possibility of adultery in our marriages, of infidelity in our relationships, drives this (perhaps unhappy) fact home. For how can we ever know everything, something, anything, about anyone else? How can we say with certainty what someone has or hasn't done? What they would or would not do?

And if we can't be sure about this, how can we be sure about anything? Just thinking about adultery plunges us into a world that has more uncertainties than certainties. Thinking about adultery is profoundly destabilizing. Which isn't always a bad thing.

Virginia Woolf made this insight clear in a marvelous little story she wrote at the end of her life called "The Legacy." (Which means, of course, that Woolf had adultery very much on her mind in the months before she died.) In the story, the central character, Gilbert Clandon, is a husband who thinks he has known his wife, Angela, very well. After her death, though, he discovers a diary she has kept throughout their long marriage.

Though she has left all her friends and acquaintances carefully wrapped presents (as if she knew she was going to die), she has left him nothing but her fifteen volumes of diary bound in green leather. It is her only legacy to him. And what a legacy it proves to be!

Her death has come as a shock to him. She has died, ostensibly, from an unfortunate accident—stepping off a curb in Piccadilly into the path of an oncoming automobile. In reading the diary, at first he is thrilled, for Angela describes how proud she was of him when they married; how she wanted to help him in his political career; how she cared deeply about making a good impression on his colleagues. She has been a good and dutiful wife, he reminisces, always putting his needs before her own.

He remembers her childishness with fondness, and how naive and adorable she had been. Flipping from one year to the next, though, he begins to encounter a mysterious figure, a man his wife calls "B. M." From the first, Angela and B. M. argue heatedly about socialism. Though Angela apparently won't permit B. M. to say anything personally condemnatory about Gilbert Clandon, still, it's clear that they discuss him and his politics derisively. Clandon surmises that B. M. was a working-class man who airs his views to women of the upper class, that he is short, stubby, poorly dressed, and unkempt.

As he reads through the last several years of the diary, Clandon sees that he himself is rarely if ever mentioned, and that B. M. is mentioned often. B. M. and his wife, he learns, have had an important relationship. They have had heated discussions of radical politics and the inequities of the class system. They have read works like Karl Marx's "The Coming Revolution" together; they have done political work in London's East End. And they have met frequently in his own home (while he has been out evenings carrying on the important business of government).

This woman whom he assumed to be naive, innocent, and passive has apparently developed an acute political sensibility and her husband hasn't even realized it, just as he hasn't noticed that she's been unfaithful to him. It is in the pages of the diary that have been heavily overwritten to disguise their contents that Clandon assumes the detailed history of Angela and B. M.'s sexual relations is recounted.

In the diary, Clandon learns that B. M. has threatened suicide if his wife didn't end her marriage and that he has, in fact, killed himself. "Have I," Angela has written, "the courage to do it too?" His wife's death, then, was no accident.

This woman whom Clandon arrogantly thought that he had known, "The Legacy" tells us, he hadn't known at all. "He had received his legacy," the story concludes. "She had told him the truth." Angela's legacy to Clandon was something Virginia Woolf believed was a bedrock principle: that human beings are fundamentally unknowable; to believe they are knowable is arrogant.

I first read this story years ago, when I was in graduate school, about the time I was recovering from my husband's affair. When I learned the circumstances under which Woolf penned it—that she wrote it near the end of her life, and that she left it for her husband Leonard Woolf to find after *her* suicide—I believed that "The Legacy" was, in its own way, a brutal, retaliatory legacy for Woolf's own husband, even though so many seem to believe that theirs was a marriage made in heaven, if not in the bedroom. And I learned, too, that writing about adultery can be an exquisite form of revenge.

For there were, at the end of her life, those volumes and volumes of diaries on Woolf's own shelves, containing, what? After reading "The Legacy," did Leonard perhaps surmise that his wife's diaries contained evidence of an unknown affair on Woolf's part?

He knew about his wife's affair with Vita Sackville-West. But he didn't know how important that love affair was to Woolf. Did Leonard search through Virginia's diaries as Clandon had flipped through his wife's, looking for Woolf's own B. M.? If he did, he learned that Sackville-West was, in many ways, the most important love of his wife's life.

Why else would Woolf write such a story at such a time? She suspected she was near the end of her life. Was she angry at Leonard, despite her protestations in her suicide notes (there were two) that he was the best of husbands? Did she suspect that Leonard had been unfaithful and so was retaliating? (We have no evidence that he was.) Was she still angry with him for denying her children? (It had been his choice, not theirs, not hers, and Angela Clandon too is childless.) For describing her as a frigid ice princess in a novel he wrote soon after their marriage that surely humiliated her and that, some say, precipitated a major breakdown? For telling everyone the sexual failure of their marriage was her fault, not theirs, and surely not his? Or was the story a work of the imagination, unconnected to Woolf or her views of marriage?

No, I think "The Legacy" was more than an innocent gesture. For although Virginia Woolf stayed married, she was one of the world's foremost critics of marriage and of the ways in which marriage forestalled freedom (at least for a woman). And I think that "The Legacy" reminded Leonard, as it reminds us even now, that we cannot claim to know the people we've married nor can we believe that they love us simply because they choose to continue to share our lives. For Virginia, of course, had had her very own B. M. in the person of Vita Sackville-West, who, not coincidentally, referred to her mother as B. M.—"Bonne Mere." And the radical politics these two discussed were feminism and socialism.

Was "The Legacy" Virginia Woolf's way of telling Leonard that her affair with Vita was the most important event in her married life? That her sexual relationship with Vita, though short-lived, was the only satisfying sex she'd had since she married? I think so.

On the subject of adultery, my husband, like the husband in "The Legacy," doesn't know what I now think. Doesn't know what I'd now do. Which is the way I want it. This doesn't mean that I *have* had an affair. Nor does it mean that I *have not* had one. I choose to admit to neither. For admitting to either tells you more about me than I'd like you to know. And admitting to either would tell my husband more about me than I'd like *him* to know. For, to me, choosing not to speak of your private life is a fundamental right we each must zealously guard even as we negotiate what it means to be responsible to our loved ones in an age of AIDS.

My husband, for example, was surprised that I wasn't furious with President Clinton when we learned precisely what he had done with Monica Lewinsky. He imagined that I would have sided with those who thought him immoral (for having affairs in the first place) and immature (for the form their sex had taken), that I would have relished Maureen Dowd's daily rantings in the *New York Times* excoriating Clinton.

But I did not. I thought he behaved admirably enough, under the circumstances. He didn't threaten his health or that of his wife. Perhaps his "affair" can be thought of as a model for acting responsibly, if one chooses to act adulterously, in our time.

Actually, the whole thing made me terribly sad and not because I felt betrayed, as so many people confessed to feeling, and not because it reminded me of my own experience all those long years ago. It made me terribly sad because the only question people seemed to be interested in having the answer to was "What was done?" not "How did everyone feel about what happened?" and not "Why might it have happened in the first place?"

I remember reading in the Kinsey report that the time of greatest adulterous sexual activity for men was after they received a job promotion. Well, Clinton had received the biggest job promotion a person could get, so he was acting true to form.

But I could also understand why someone with no freedom whatsoever and no privacy at all would want to try to reclaim the ability to do whatever he chose to do whenever he chose to do it and at whatever cost. Which, I think, is fundamentally what adultery is all about. Adultery is and always has been about reclaiming an *autonomy* lost to us through marriage. Adultery is about saying, through our actions, that, regardless of who I am, of what vows I have taken, of what responsibilities I have (and especially *because* of the responsibilities I have), I have the right to do whatsoever I choose so long as I don't harm anyone. (That adultery inevitably harms another seems never to be taken into consideration.)

Autonomy. This is probably why my husband had his affair when he did. And why so many doctors-in-training seem (at least in my experience) to have so many affairs. Adultery to me is always, in part, an act of desperation, a way of claiming that life is still worth living when it seems that, though we've gotten what we've wanted, we've lost more in the process than we've gained.

Let's face it. Clinton may be Commander in Chief. But he can't slip into Po in Greenwich Village for some of the most exquisite Italian food outside Italy like I can almost any time I want to. And he can't cruise the aisles of Barnes and Noble and pick up *The Story of O* or *Lady Chatterley's Lover*, or *Vox*, say, without the whole world knowing about it. He can't pick his nose in public or fight with his wife or yell at his daughter for doing something stupid. He can't fart or touch his dick (in public). Can't go anywhere, not even across the street, without it being a VERY BIG DEAL.

Poor bastard. Many people envy his power. I have always felt sorry for him, felt sorry for every public figure. As my mother used to say, there are only two tragedies in life: getting what you've always wanted, and not getting what you've always wanted. Clinton got what he wanted. He got to be President. And, to me, his actions tell us he is dying of sorrow.

(The day after I write this, I think it's too wild, I'll have to delete it. On impulse, though, I click onto AOL and access the transcripts of the Monica

Lewinsky/Linda Tripp telephone conversations. And find this.

Bill Clinton to Monica Lewinsky: "I have an empty life." Monica Lewinsky to Linda Tripp: "I think he likes to feel sorry for himself." There is some talk, too, of how Air Force One and hearing "Hail to the Chief" and the parties and receptions and all the trappings that accompany being president have become routine. That the President of the United States believes his life is empty and that he feels sorry for himself might merit some discussion on our part.)

Anyway. To return to my adultery story. Some time after my husband confessed his affair to me, I looked into the bathroom mirror and thought that I might kill myself or that I would go back to graduate school and become economically independent as quickly as I could. This might sound like a strange set of choices for someone to have in such circumstances, but I can assure you that they presented themselves to my consciousness in precisely this way.

I looked into the bathroom mirror. I saw my ravaged face. My swollen eyes. It was a face I didn't recognize. It was the face of a wounded woman. I didn't want this face. I didn't want to be this woman.

I wondered whether I could kill myself by taking a year's supply of birth control pills (the gift of some pharmaceutical company to the spouses of interns)—

they were the only stash of pills I had in the house.
I figured, though, that the way my luck was running,
I might grow some hair on my chest, but that I probably wouldn't die. Even in such a desperate moment,
my sense of humor hadn't deserted me. So I decided I
would go back to graduate school, get a Ph.D., and
become a college professor.

I decided that if my husband chose to stay married,
I would stay married. But that in my heart I would be
as free as if I weren't married at all. For the rest of my
marriage.

I wanted, I realized, not just a job, but a *real* career,
something that would lead me to a grand intellectual
(and perhaps another kind of) passion. Staying stuck
in my apartment wasn't the way to reclaim my life.
Leaving our baby home with a baby-sitter, or with my
husband or a grandparent, driving into New York
City, taking courses at New York University (where
I'd earlier taken some summer graduate courses),
hanging out in Washington Square, might, I thought,
help me reclaim my life, though it might not save my
marriage.

Slowly I started to regain my lost self. Like the
heroine in Fay Weldon's *Life and Loves of a She-Devil*,
I broke all the rules about how you were supposed to
act if you were a woman in my situation. I called
everyone I knew, including his parents and mine, and
told them my husband was fucking around. I asked

them for financial help until I could start supporting myself. I started my own bank account which he didn't know about. Stashed money whenever I could—my long-range goal: to have a year's worth of expenses so I could leave my marriage at any time should I need to.

Meantime, I thought I might temporarily squelch the young-doctor-leaves-his-young-wife-for-nurse script by telling my husband that if he left me, *he* could have the baby. *He* could figure out how to have a romantic life with a squalling baby who always threw up. This made him stick around for awhile.

This "tough broad" tone I take is, of course, a cover for how hurt I then was, for how betrayed I felt. Strangely, I never remember feeling jealous. Knowing that your spouse has had (is having) an affair provides an education in tolerating feelings of betrayal, helplessness, hopelessness, shame, and loneliness. I thought I had done everything the way you were supposed to—clipped coupons, supported him through medical school (financially and otherwise), made casseroles with noodles and chopped meat and cream of mushroom soup. And still my husband wanted to leave me. I later learned that even if you do whatever you're supposed to do your husband can leave you, so you may as well do whatever you want.

But this also provided an opportunity for me to learn that however much we may believe we mean them, marital vows are meaningless for we can't predict the future nor control it. We are inevitably, each of us, alone and the sooner we learn this, the better off we are.

There was something exhilarating, too, about knowing that my husband had been untrue: it permitted me to think about what I really wanted for myself, about the person I wanted to become, about the life I wanted to lead. When he came home from work, I no longer necessarily stopped reading my book. When he came home from work, I no longer necessarily was home.

I really don't know what I would have done if my husband *had* left me. Don't know if I could have given up my son. Unlike many of our friends, my husband decided to stay, and I decided to let him stay.

Though it might well be true that my husband's lover wasn't a nurse, I still swear that that's what he told me when I found out that he was fooling around. I have never before typed those words—"my husband's lover"—and I don't like them. Still I can't think what else to call her. I know they fucked, so perhaps I should say, my husband's *fuckee*.

But maybe he never told me what she was and it's just what I assumed because so many other women married to the men in my husband's medical school class got dumped for nurses, often after working for years to support them through their training. Maybe

I simply *imagined* that my story was the same story as their story. (And adultery stories are really basically all the same, even though as you're telling them you think that they're startlingly original. Honestly. Is there anything more trying than the conversation of a friend in the process of having an adulterous affair? And is there anything more exciting than telling such a story?)

I know for a fact, though, that she was gorgeous. Once, when he was in the thick of his affair—it's what I always say to describe this time in our lives *when Ernie was in the thick of his affair with that nurse*—I rifled through his wallet while he was taking a shower. It is something I'd never done before and something I've never done since.

We were in some cheap motel in Georgetown trying to patch up our marriage (at least *I* was trying to patch up our marriage; he might have come along just because he didn't know how to say no or out of guilt or general bewilderment).

When I reached into the little pocket in his wallet where he normally carried pictures of his parents, of me (taken at a prenuptial splurge at Trader Vic's), and of our infant son, I found, instead, just one picture. A picture of her.

She was strawberry blonde and looked something like Grace Kelly. She was, unlike me, very fair, very unethnic, very, very un-Italian. I knew I was in trou-

ble because she looked something like a blonde unavailable girl my husband had longed for but never
dated in high school. She too had masses of light-col-
ored curls piled on the top of her head. Those days,
I was lucky if I got the time to pull a comb through
my sensible, extremely short, extremely dark hair.
Unlike me, she was beautifully though lavishly made
up. ("No matter how tired you are, always change
your clothes and put on some makeup before he comes
home from work," my mother-in-law advised me
soon after I gave birth. "It's what I do for Don." But
my husband wasn't coming home all that often, and
when he did, I was so hurt and bewildered and pissed
off at him that makeup was the furthest thing from
my mind.)

Great, I thought to myself as I slipped her picture
back into his wallet. *He's fucking around because
he wants to feel the way he used to feel in high school.
Lovesick.*

Adultery, I realized then, I still think now, is very,
very adolescent. It's when a grown person tries to
feel the way they did when they were in love in high
school. Knowing this, though, didn't help my circumstances at all. For I knew the addictive pleasure of
adolescent sex; I had had more great sex during my
adolescence than many people have during a lifetime.

On the back of the photo, in a girlish backhand,
the words "Love, always" preceded her name which,

fortunately for her, I have blocked, for if I remembered it, I would have to decide whether I wanted to use it or not, and probably, to respect her privacy, I wouldn't, though I might want to. Probably I'd decide to change her name.

I'm sure she had compelling reasons for doing what she did. Maybe she really loved him. Maybe she saw him as a good catch. I know she had a daughter and perhaps she thought her daughter should have a father. Only my husband was already someone's father. Though not yet a very good one.

So that we could take the trip that was supposed to help us patch up our marriage, my parents volunteered to care for our son, the one he now says he'd never leave.

He is wrong, I am sure, about that. Because I remember at least one very tense (actually totally hysterical) conversation about the possibility of his leaving us in the living room of our apartment in Cranford, New Jersey, with the baby crying in his crib in his bedroom, and me staring at the fringe of our blood-red carpet to steady myself because I felt sure I was falling into a giant hole from which there was no possible escape.

The carpet was one that I was proud of possessing because I had gotten it as a remnant on sale at a local carpet store and persuaded the proprietor to have it bound and fringed for a pittance. I was a good money manager then; I am a good money manager now. Then we were trying to subsist on my husband's three thousand dollars a year—what interns earned in those days when everyone assumed doctors came from the privileged class—and an allowance from his parents. I had given up my job to take care of our baby the way that women sometimes do because they believe it is their duty or because they believe it will be rewarding (and sometimes, I suppose, it can be, though that surely wasn't my experience). I went from being a respected teacher to being an anxious mother and an ignored housewife.

I remember asking my husband through shuddering sobs how he could possibly think of leaving us, his son wasn't even six months old and he needed a father. I remember that I went raging into the nursery to get the crying baby to shove in front of his face as Demonstration A of "The Baby You Are Going to Leave Behind to Be with That Woman."

In a moment that seemed scripted for daytime television (which I am ashamed to admit I had, in my desperation, begun watching), I remember holding the baby up to him and asking him how he felt about abandoning his own flesh and blood. I also remember telling him that if he left, he could take the baby with him. I didn't plan to be young, single, a mother, and on welfare.

He said he didn't believe I could give our baby up.

By now, I had stopped crying and was all steely reserve, and I said, "Wanna bet?"

This primal scene, I feel sure, has been deeply implanted in the psyche of our child, who is now a man, with a child of his own, though perhaps he doesn't remember it. We know, for example, that when babies in utero hear people laughing, they sometimes smile. Even inside their mother's body, they are affected by the emotional climate that surrounds them. My son's body, his spirit, his soul, I am sure, have been scarred by this dreadful time in our lives. And I regret, Ernie regrets this, more than anything about our experience.

As I said before, my mother and father had agreed to take care of our son so that we could go on our little holiday to Georgetown. It had been my mother's idea. She believed that if I could have a short holiday with my husband, it might save our marriage. Especially, as my mother reminded me, if I was nice to him, made sure we had a good time together, and didn't mention his affair.

"Sooner or later *she'll* start bitching and moaning to him every time she sees him," a friend whose own marriage had nearly fallen apart told me. "Let *her* be the pain in the ass while you remain an oasis of calm."

An oasis of calm. I remember those words even now. I should make my home into an oasis of calm, even as my husband was firing heavy artillery at me at point-blank range. Nonetheless I tried. And seemed to have succeeded.

When I dropped off our son at my parents' house before our holiday, my mother, never one to counsel me, because she knew me well enough to know that I *never* did what she suggested, took the baby out of my arms, and the diaper bag, and the small piece of luggage holding his clothes. She looked straight into my eyes (something that she rarely did, for she was a woman who seemed always to glance sideways at the world). And she uttered just one sentence of advice that I did, in fact, take, though taking it meant that I had to do something that I would have preferred, under the circumstances, not to have to do.

"Sleep with him," she said. "Even if it's hard for you. Even if it makes you cry."

And reader, I *did* fuck him. And it was hard for me, and it did make me weep.

Four

These days, when people ask me what I'm working on, and I tell them that I'm writing a book about adultery, they look at me disgustedly or quizzically or sardonically or bemusedly. Sometimes they groan. Sometimes they chuckle. Sometimes they roll their eyes. Sometimes they shake their head. Sometimes they walk away. And I can't blame them. For they think that I am jumping on a very popular contemporary bandwagon.

These days, adultery, after all, is not a highly original topic. (Actually, it's never been highly original. Alfred S. Kinsey says that it is the most significant and popular subject in the world's literature.) Without the tug of current events, they think, adultery can't possibly be something I'd voluntarily chosen to write about. The subject, they think, preoccupies me because of my own experience. I didn't choose the subject. I am compelled to write about it.

When I say I'm writing a book about adultery, sometimes the men I'm talking to look straight into my eyes and leer, as if I couldn't have a purely academic interest in my subject (and perhaps I don't). This is something I'm not used to because I am not the kind of woman that ever attracted a man's attention unless I chose to. I never tossed my hair and tilted my head to one side and acted coy and simpered to indicate that I was available to anyone who wanted me. I was always too busy for such nonsense. Reading. Writing. Taking care of a family. Building an academic career. Caring about really serious topics.

Sometimes the men I'm talking to ask me if I'm writing a memoir. When they say the word *memoir* they smile, slightly, they can't help themselves. They smile, I imagine, because they are imagining me in some seedy motel room furnished with a sagging bed, an ugly chenille spread, a cheap print of a sylvan stream, an orange plastic chair (covered with a jumble of disordered clothes, his and mine), a Formica end table with a Gideon Bible in the drawer, my legs up in the air, some guy's face "down there" or my legs wrapped around the thick waist of—hmm—who could it have been? They ask me if I have any *personal* —they purse their lips as they say the word making it seem like saying it is an illicit kiss they're giving me—

interest in the subject. I tell them I do, but not for the reasons they think.

When I mention that I am writing a book about adultery, the woman I am talking to usually says "Oh, how interesting," and excuses herself, and walks away.

I have been trying to understand adultery for much of my life, and bumping up against it throughout my life, and in the strangest places, and writing about it, sometimes without anticipating it, for many years. For whenever I have seriously studied a writer's life, I have invariably encountered at least one important adultery story. Adultery, it seems to me, is a critical emotional experience in many of our lives. But not many of us talk about it, not many of us acknowledge it, not many of us have taken the time to understand the lessons it can teach.

I start a book in the early seventies about how Virginia Woolf wrote her first novel, *The Voyage Out*. I am primarily interested in the creative process. A few days into my research, I discover that Virginia Woolf's flirtatious (if indeed not overtly adulterous) relationship with her sister's husband is a primary emotional source for that novel. Later, I discover, too, that Woolf's adulterous lesbian relationship with Vita Sackville-West was a life-changing experience for them both—Woolf discovered she wasn't frigid, that she wasn't as "crazy" as she thought; Sackville-West discovered that her capacities as a writer were far greater than she imagined. Each of their marriages profited from their mutual, long-lasting love.

I start a paper about Djuna Barnes's creation of her dramatic masterpiece, *The Antiphon*. I am primarily interested in her creative process, in the fact that she is an incest survivor and whether she transmuted that experience into her art. A few days into my research, I learn that a central formative experience in Barnes's life, which she describes in her best-selling novel *Ryder*, was the impact of her father's adultery. For Barnes's father brought his lover home, and the situation strained the limits of Barnes's remarkable capacities of coping with what had been a horrifically abusive family and probably contributed to her breakdown.

I begin rereading Henry Miller's works for a book I'm writing about him. And learn that the event that changed Miller's life and scorched his soul and that prompted the writing of *Tropic of Cancer* and every other novel he wrote, was the adultery of his second wife, June, who eloped to Paris with her female lover.

I begin reading about Colette. For pleasure. For I am traveling to the part of France she wrote about. And learn that her husband Willy's blatant infidelities changed her forever and affected her writing for the rest of her life.

Louise DeSalvo   *Adultery*

I begin rereading D. H. Lawrence's works for a book I'm writing about him. And quickly learn that Lawrence's tortured conflict between desiring sexual fidelity and living in an extremely adulterous marriage formed the bedrock of every novel he penned after *The Rainbow.*

Through the years, I have come to see infidelity and adultery, not as moral issues, but rather as ways of understanding the complicated nature of people's *desire.* "Love," Thomas Moore has written in *Care of the Soul,* "asks many things of us, including actions that seem to be utterly counter to feelings of attachment and loyalty." The shadow sides of attachment and loyalty—independence and infidelity—paradoxically, says Moore, "may ultimately bring the love to its proper, if mysterious and unpredictable home."

This certainly is true for me. For unless we experience the shadow side of love, our experience in loving will necessarily be incomplete. We will love shallowly, sentimentally, selfishly. We will expect our love to meet impossible ideals, unreal expectations. "Disappointments in love, even betrayals and losses," says Moore, "serve the soul at the very moment they seem in life to be tragedies."

Confronting adultery and infidelity always means that we must examine uncharted emotional territory; that we must open ourselves to new definitions of who we are, of who we might become; that we must see our partners' needs as differing from our own.

For so often in committed relationships, we refuse to deal with the complexity that is the other person. We can't understand the reasons that compel her to seek affection elsewhere. We retreat to the position of the wounded child, of the morally offended. It is, after all, easier to feel hurt than to feel responsible for understanding what has happened and what it can teach us. This, though, can lead to discoveries about the other person, and about ourselves and human nature.

At the very least, infidelity means that someone is trying to get you to notice that s/he is not the person that you think s/he is. Infidelity means that someone is trying to get you to notice that you are not the person s/he thought you were. That we are all protean.

Henry Miller often spoke of using what he called the "jujitsu of human emotions"—allowing ourselves to move *with* someone else's power when we are seriously threatened, rather than remaining intractable. To cure the self in a relationship in which our partner has been unfaithful necessitates that we become what the other person has become—not an adulterer per se, but a person who loosens her or his limitations; a person who is willing to change; a person who accepts change as inevitable; a person who is willing to establish profound connections with people beyond the family; a person who is willing to take

Louise DeSalvo *Adultery*

time for private pleasure; a person who is able to experience life erotically.

As our partner has been drawn to the libertine life, so, too, can we be. If our partner has been unfaithful to us, perhaps it is because we have been unfaithful to ourselves. For if we couple with someone who is unfaithful, perhaps they are enacting our own hidden desires. Perhaps we can allow ourselves to explore unfamiliar emotional territory; to become deeper and more authentic.

Facing adultery shatters the illusion of safety and predictability that generally comes when we're in a committed relationship. And this troubles most people. (It surely troubled me.) It forced me to realize that thinking myself a part of a couple was illusive, that each of us really exists in the world alone, though we can share moments of deep communion. These insights, though, are necessary to forge a mature working partnership rather than remaining in an infantile romanticized union. I now never want to be in a relationship so significant, so centrally important to my life, that I would say, "Without him, I would die."

If this sounds terribly cynical, it isn't. It is, instead, I think, deeply realistic. I find a heady sense of freedom and independence from this realization. My view is that too many people expect too much from their relationships and their marriages and they're chronically critical of their mates and disillusioned because they're not getting what they think they deserve or what they know they need. But, after all, why do we believe we are entitled to have someone else give us what we can't give ourselves? This, I believe, is the most unfortunate aspect of a romanticized view of marriage: making your partner responsible for your happiness.

Knowing that my marriage nearly ended once has made me value it more because I value it less and I value myself more. I know that being with my husband is an ongoing, freely chosen, shape-shifting process on both our parts, which we sometimes negotiate well, and sometimes, not well at all. Each day, we both have to redefine our commitment to our relationship and what it means to us right now, given the changing circumstances of our lives.

I have often been asked how I could have forgiven my husband, or why. I always reply that what he did didn't require forgiveness; it merited understanding, even empathy. His adultery signaled a challenge to our marriage; it didn't mean its end (unless he or I or we chose to end it). In time, I discovered that a contrite husband makes a wonderful partner, and that most long relationships include an episode like the one we have lived through, and that dwelling on past pain robs us of the magic of the present moment.

I love what the wife in Gabriel García Márquez's *Love in the Time of Cholera* understands after her sometime unfaithful husband has died. She marvels at how it was possible over time to have been so content when, daily in her marriage, she has been involved in so many arguments and so many annoyances. One reason is her understanding that everything changes, that everything that is pleasant contains the possibility of pain. That everything that is painful contains the possibility of joy.

What my husband did spurred me to growth, to finding what I wanted, what I had always wanted and to satisfying myself.

Though you surely don't choose to have the experience I had, you can nonetheless control how you respond to it. I chose not to be the kind of person who rifles through a spouse's possessions, who sniffs at clothing, who queries absences, who opens mail, who listens in on extensions. I chose to eliminate suspicion (for the most part) from my life. I chose not to become as obsessed about adultery as the heroine in Donna Masini's brilliant novel, *About Yvonne*, which charts the madness we invite when we choose to pry into our partner's love affairs. (Anyone who is so tempted should read this work.)

I chose my response because I do not want to be in a relationship where anyone opens my mail, listens in on my telephone calls, rifles through my possessions, queries my absences. I too want my freedom and my autonomy.

My experience told me that I needed to think about adultery differently. I thought I believed that having sex with someone other than your lawful partner necessarily ruined a marriage. Actually, I borrowed this assumption from the cultural imperative that this be so. But this wasn't honestly true for me. I didn't care about the sex. What I cared about, truly, was that he seemed to be having a good time with someone else and I wasn't having a good time with anyone. Later, much later, I learned that having an affair isn't necessarily always fun, and that it often isn't fun at all. However difficult the experience we encountered, my marriage—and I—were better off because of what Ernie had done.

In Plato's *Symposium*, Socrates is instructed by a wise woman, Diotima of Mantineia, about the nature of love. She tells him that people often think incorrectly about love. Love, she says, is not always associated with pleasure, although people erroneously believe that it should be, and that if it is not, that love has vanished, and the relationship should be terminated. There is, for example, Diotima reminds Socrates, the difficulty of childbirth, the worry of raising children, the inevitability of the changing nature of human relationships, and the loss of loved ones.

All these experiences, though they are worthwhile and often pleasurable, are often painful, even sorrowful. And their pain and sorrow are essential to the deepening of love which remains egotistical and infantile unless it endures these obstacles.

Love, Diotima insists, is "a philosopher or lover of wisdom." And love, and the difficulties of loving, perhaps, are our greatest teachers. What loving teaches us, she believes, are ongoing lessons about the everlasting nature of change and our inability to always control our destiny, though we can control our response to it.

Through contemplating the inevitable transformations that occur in any human relationship, we become humbled, but we also become wise. We learn to yield. We learn to witness ourselves as pliant and resourceful. For as Thomas Moore has written, "If we can honor love as it presents itself, taking shapes and directions we would never have predicted or desired, then we are on the way toward discovering the lower levels of soul, where meaning and value reveal themselves slowly and paradoxically."

On the night that I found out that my husband was having an affair, I grabbed the keys to his car (I didn't have one at the time; we were too poor to afford two, too poor even, to afford one, but his parents were helping us out), ran down the stairs, and jumped into the car. I drove it very far and very fast, half hoping that I wasn't an expert enough driver to keep the speeding car on the road. I'd double-clutched and downshifted our Mustang skillfully through the hair-pin turns of coastal highways in California during an idyllic summer holiday we'd taken a few years before. I had excellent reflexes and I was a fast and sure driver so I don't believe that I was in any real danger. Still, it was difficult to see the road through my tears; difficult, too, to keep my mind on my driving.

I had no destination in mind, really, though I headed north, in the direction of the Palisades Interstate Parkway. The "solace road" we used to call it in high school, for my friends and I often drove that beautiful, winding, tree-lined highway overlooking the Hudson River when we were desperately unhappy. We often paused to park at one or another of the lookouts off that road from which you could see the George Washington Bridge or Riverdale, to contemplate our lives or to have a good cry.

These parking lots held a special significance for us; they were where we often went to park and neck or make love. I knew that I needed to be alone for a long time to gather my thoughts, to sort things out, and there was no better place to do this than in such a familiar place. A place where Roy and I went when I was in high school, and later, with Ernie, after we started dating.

Hours passed. Night changed to dawn. I thought of leaving. I thought of telling Ernie to leave. I thought of staying. I thought of asking him to stay. Yet I realized that I would choose not to act, at least not yet. I would watch and I would wait. All through that long night, I kept remembering Roy, and thinking about my love affair with him helped me understand my husband's, for I knew the powerful tug of having a clandestine lover.

As I pulled back onto the highway, heading home, I thought to myself, *It will be interesting to see what happens.*

This was a line I'd borrowed in high school as a kind of personal credo from Sloan Wilson's *The Man in the Grey Flannel Suit*. The central character, Thomas R. Rath, utters this line the moment before he parachutes behind enemy lines in the Pacific during World War II. He has no choice about doing this. He is neither brave nor cowardly. He is simply human, and he would prefer not to live through something he must nonetheless experience. But he gathers courage by approaching this terrifying event with deep curiosity as I now hoped to.

I had once read a parable about a Zen monk about to be devoured by a lion who, in the moments before his terrible death, pauses to notice the beauty of a flower blooming nearby. That's what I wanted, too, for myself: to live in the fullness and potential of the present moment, whatever life's circumstances. This was not something I had accomplished; it was a way of life to which I aspired.

Although this may suggest a passive approach to life, to me "It will be interesting to see what happens" has always meant a watchful appreciation of whatever I would need to live through, no matter how difficult or painful the experience. And I would have my share of them in the future: my sister's suicide; my mother's long and painful dying; a serious injury; a serious illness. Living through these times with attention, and respecting difficulties as an inevitable part of a rich life (rather than wishing them away, which is to wish life away), has become a habit of being for me.

I'd read Sloan Wilson's novel soon after it was published in the mid-fifties. It was a novel about adultery, but I don't think that's why I read it, though what it had to say about adultery meant much to me because it was so sensible. For in the novel, an adultery doesn't mean the end of a marriage, though it surely complicates it. Rather, it signals a new beginning for both wife and husband.

I think I appreciated its message because I was reading it after the mother of someone I knew killed herself, we were told, because she suspected that her husband was cheating on her. (As it turned out, she was correct.) This seemed to me, even then, too radical an act in response to the collapse of a marriage. I never wanted a man to mean that much to me that his leaving me would mean that I would think that my life was over. Even then, perhaps because of my working-class background, perhaps because of my fantasies about my grandfather, I saw the ideal marriage less as a romantic relationship, less as a way of fulfilling all of our heart's desires, and more as a working partnership with a person whom you respected.

I was first drawn to *The Man in the Grey Flannel Suit,* though, not because it was about adultery, but because it was described as a realistic portrait of combat in the Pacific during World War II, where my father had spent years during the war. I wanted to learn why my father was so difficult to live with, why he flew off the handle so readily, why, as my mother always said, he came back from that war a changed man. I had to learn about my father's life during the war the only way I knew how—by reading about what he might have experienced—because my father wasn't talking. So I read *The Man in the Grey Flannel Suit* to find out.

And I *did* learn about my father through reading about Wilson's hero, Thomas R. Rath. He, too, had his rages—has thrown a cut-glass vase at a wall where it leaves a permanent mark as testimony to his propensity for violence. He, too, can't seem to find meaning in postwar life. He, too, wants a wonderful house, a dutiful wife, and a perfect no-problem family to justify what he's lived through. He, too, doesn't talk about the war and can't express his feelings. We understand, though, through graphic flashbacks, about the dehumanizing horror of nighttime hand-to-hand combat, the loss of treasured comrades, the stress of never knowing when or where your next battle will be fought, of never knowing whether you'll live to see the next dawn, or whether you'll ever return home.

But I learned, too, an attitude toward adultery that helped me immeasurably when I faced the crisis in my own marriage. For Sloan Wilson has scripted the aftermath of adultery differently from the tragedies and sorrows I'd encountered in so many novels about adultery I'd previously read. Anna Karenina's throwing herself under a train; Madame Bovary's ingesting the arsenic that kills her; Hester Prynne living her loveless, dutiful life on the fringes of a community that grudgingly comes to accept her.

In Wilson's novel, adultery doesn't mean the end of a marriage and so it posits a radical solution to the dilemma of adultery. A narrative like this, Alfred S. Kinsey observes in *Sexual Behavior in the Human Male*, challenges traditional thinking because the adultery narrative that society seems to prefer is the one that ends in disaster. Perhaps the nearly universal tragic adultery narrative serves to keep our nearly universal desire for the adulterous experience in check, for Kinsey discovered that most people admitted they would be unfaithful if they never were discovered.

In *The Man in the Grey Flannel Suit*, Thomas R.

Rath has had an adulterous love affair with Maria, a young woman, during the war, while he waits in Italy to be sent to the Pacific. With her, he spends the tension-filled weeks before he is shipped out. When he leaves, he learns that she is pregnant. Years later, he discovers that she has had a child, that they are destitute and need help.

Although he initially believes he can forget this experience, he learns that he can't. In thinking about it, he realizes that he must honor it. He knows that loving this woman was a necessary antidote to all the death he had seen. His being with her, he understands, was the only good thing that happened to him during the war. And his infidelity, he feels sure, has had nothing to do with his love for his wife.

In time he finds that he must tell his wife about what happened because he wants to support his child, because it is the right and just thing to do, and he doesn't want to do it without his wife's knowledge. Unlike scores of other men who have abandoned the children they've fathered during the war, Rath honors his obligation, though it means testing his marriage.

He tells his wife what Maria has meant to him and why he has lived with her. He refuses to minimize the relationship's importance or to speak poorly of Maria. What he's done, he insists, isn't despicable; it's human. The meaning of his action must be integrated into both their lives.

Betsy Rath ultimately comes to believe that learning about her husband's wartime experience can enrich their love rather than destroy it, though initially she feels angry and betrayed. For she must abandon the chimera of a perfect union for the challenge of living in a flawed but real relationship that can be enriched by their mutual history. As he tells her what he's lived through, so she tells him what it has felt like to live through the war without knowing whether he was dead or alive. The novel ends with their commitment to inscribing for themselves a new kind of relationship beyond their culture's rigid definitions of what marital fidelity means.

After I learned about my husband's affair, I wanted to act like Betsy Rath in Wilson's novel, despite what people were telling me about how I should act, despite some desperate moments of my own—one, when I nearly succumbed to a knee-jerk, inauthentic, self-destructive response to what happened that I have earlier described. For it was extremely difficult to respond as I wanted, in the face of how others expected me to behave.

I was told, for example, that if I had any self-respect, I'd kick the bastard out. That if what happened to me happened to them, they would pack up all his clothes and give them to Goodwill; they would change the locks on the doors; they would call a lawyer. I was told by one person that I should hunt them down and run them over with our car; she seemed serious when she said this. Another suggested that I get a gun and find them and shoot them; I hope she didn't mean it. When I told one friend that I didn't necessarily want to end my marriage, she told me she couldn't possibly continue our relationship because I obviously was a masochist; she never spoke to me again; our friendship ended. Another woman said she'd start returning my calls when I showed her I knew the meaning of revenge.

In those early days after I learned about my husband's affair, I realized how desperately people want you to act according to *their* expectations of what should happen in the wake of adultery. They want tragedy. They insist upon public scenes and recriminations. They want families to split up; children to be fought over; men to rage; women to weep. Most did not want what I gave them: an angry yet pensive and most certainly private pause in a relationship I chose not to end. A rethinking and reassessment of our marriage and my place in it. Another set of ground rules, a new beginning, a moving on.

People insist that adultery be a public spectacle instead of remaining a private matter. If there is anything my experience, and the Clinton debacle, has taught me, it is this: for whatever reason, when people smell adultery, they want a nasty show. And if you refuse to give it to them, because it's not your style, or because you value yourself more than you value your marriage, or because you insist on privacy, or because you think that it's your business not theirs, they get pissed, they get vindictive, and they attack. They want your marriage to be what they think marriage should be; they want how you wrestle with the aftermath of adultery to match society's norms.

Maureen Dowd, writing in the *New York Times*, wants to know why, in the wake of the Monica Lewinsky affair, Hillary Clinton looks so good, acts so sure, and, most especially, why she isn't wringing her hands in public (or perhaps even smacking the President of the United States over the head with her pocketbook on prime time TV). Maureen Dowd thinks that because Hillary Clinton isn't grieving publicly, she's not grieving at all, that because she isn't ranting and raving, she doesn't have any self respect. Maureen Dowd wants Hillary Clinton to do what she thinks any woman who is cheated on (we're called *cuckqueans*, I recently learned from a William Safire column in the *Times*) ought to do.

Not many people, though, want to learn what you really want. Not many people know how hard it is to assess your life and make good choices that you must live with when you're feeling so wounded, when everyone is telling you what to do, when everyone is morally assessing your every move and finding it wanting.

Louise DeSalvo *Adultery*

My mother-in-law did want to know what I wanted to do. She asked me. I told her I wanted my marriage. She listened. She helped me by taking care of my child (as my mother did too) so I could have time to think, to feel, to cry, to sleep. She provided much during a difficult time when most everyone I knew withdrew from me.

What I wanted, at first, was to understand why my husband needed to have this relationship. What my mother-in-law suggested is that I couldn't know, that I might never know, and that he probably didn't know. This, she told me, might remain one of life's mysteries. Still, in *The Man in the Grey Flannel Suit*, Betsy Rath learned that her husband's adultery had something to do with his terror. And that his relationship with Maria was an antidote to all the killing he'd seen, to all the killing he'd done. So, too, I believed that maybe so many (male and female) doctors I knew were having affairs because being an intern wasn't unlike being in combat. And that maybe, too, Ernie's adultery had something to do with a sorrow he had experienced early in life which he hadn't shared with me. Adultery, I thought, might be related to some other sorrows that we've experienced in life.

Years later, I learned that there was some truth to my assessment. People living in an atmosphere in which they are constantly threatened, constantly challenged, Allan Mazur and Alan Booth have discovered, have elevated testosterone levels, which decreases the likelihood of monogamy and increases the likelihood of polygamy. (High testosterone levels in birds predict absentee fathers and dedicated polygamists.)

This is perhaps why Ernie seemed far more inclined to monogamy before he became a doctor than after. And why I had more than one relationship during my teenage years when I lived with the threat of my father's violence. This is also perhaps why so many women, when they enter the so-called male professions, also become disinclined to monogamy. And why I myself seriously flirted with infidelity through the years I aggressively pursued tenure and a writing career.

We might all be doing nothing more, nothing less, than responding to elevated hormonal levels, which are themselves responding to ongoing, unrelenting challenge. In this context, how can we possibly expect a chronically besieged head of state to be anything but polygamous?

I do wish I had known that when men have affairs, they want to allow themselves to be vulnerable and dependent and that when women have affairs, they want to be strong and free. (This according to Annette Lawson's *Adultery*.) In affairs, each gender wants to live the possibilities foreclosed to them in "normal" marriages—women seek autonomy; men seek intimacy. Which suggests that if a marriage accommodates these behaviors, there will, perhaps, be less reason to stray.

I wish I had known that almost all species on Earth (90%), that almost all mammals (97%) are promiscuous, and that very few (only 3%) are truly monogamous. I wish I had known that certain birds (not the wattled jacana—the female is promiscuous while the male raises the offspring), however, and even certain species of mice are more likely to be truly sexually monogamous than people (according to Deborah Blum's *Sex on the Brain*).

If Ernie had been, say, a Canadian goose instead of a human being, we wouldn't have lived through this experience. But because Ernie and I are human beings, it was highly likely that this would happen. I wish I would have known this so I wouldn't have taken what happened so personally. (The chances vary greatly depending upon the source: as high as 66% for men, from a study by Shere Hite, and 54% for women, from a survey by *Cosmopolitan*.)

I wish I had known that anthropologists believe that human beings are neither completely monogamous nor completely polygamous. (Ordinary people, I think, might have some trouble swallowing this.) Scientists, it seems, can't decide whether, as a species, we are quasi-monogamous or quasi-polygamous. Anthropologist Bobbi Low, for example, says we are "slightly polygamous"; Deborah Blum, though, believes we are "ambiguously monogamous," and that we are slowly moving away from the more polygamous habits of our evolutionary ancestors.

And it does matter, I think. For, if we are quasi-polygamous, infidelity is more "normal" than fidelity; monogamy (when it occurs) is aberrant. But if we are quasi-monogamous, fidelity is more "normal"; infidelity (when it occurs) is the less "natural" behavior.

Whichever way it is, though, it is helpful to know that the drive to promiscuity seems to be genetically encoded. Perhaps knowing this might incline us to be less judgmental of those who stray. Committing adultery is something like temporarily losing your mind, something like letting instinct overtake your reason.

That's what someone I knew told me when she was in the thick of an affair that made no sense to her at all. Instead of wearing an *A* on her breast like Hester Prynne, she told me, she should have worn a scarlet *S* for *Stupid*.

How else to explain that seemingly perfectly rational human beings have been adulterous even in societies that punish adultery with castrations, amputations, stoning, exile, even death? How else to explain that otherwise perfectly respectable human beings take insane risks to have a sexual experience that (if the truth were to be told) is probably less satisfying (though it might be more exciting) than the one they can have legally and safely at home?

Perhaps adultery makes evolutionary sense: perhaps it is a pesky way our species guarantees its survival. But just try using that as an excuse if you get caught and see where it gets you: "Dear, I apologize, but you see, I was just trying to widen the chances that I would pass on my genetic material."

Actually, according to Blum, monogamy *really* only means a "greatly reduced promiscuity." In this sense, then, human beings as a species can be thought to be monogamous. Ernie's promiscuity was, most assuredly, "greatly reduced"—he was sleeping with only two of us at the same time and not sixteen of us.

I wish I had known that another meaning of monogamy (this, too, according to Blum) is who you spend most of your time with, who you raise your children with, not who you sleep with. The rodent known as the prairie vole, for example, is considered monogamous because, although they sleep around, they raise children together. On a "cool evening, [they] can be found sitting side by side."

In this sense, then, Ernie, even during the thick of his affair, was monogamous. He and I were raising our child together. And on most (though surely not all) of the evenings he wasn't working, we could be found sitting side by side, albeit (for many months) some-what sullenly.

I wish I had known that only monogamous species build "solid, and even equal male-female partnerships"

(Blum). So it is the building of the *partnership,* then, not necessarily the shared sexuality nor the incidental infidelity, that determines whether a relationship is considered monogamous.

Sexual monogamy, then, is an ideal state toward which many of us aspire but which most of us do not achieve. A monogamous *partnership,* though, *is* something that many of us can achieve, and whether we have it or not is not necessarily determined by our sexual behavior. One partner's sleeping with someone else, therefore, need not end a working partnership if you don't want that working partnership to end—as I did not.

In time, I understood that my husband's infidelity (and my reflecting on it, and the information it provided me about us and our marriage) saved our marriage. For it needed changing to become a vital union. I had to change. He had to change. His infidelity was perhaps the symptom of what needed altering.

Before our marriage and parenthood, when Ernie and I met, I had been independent, autonomous, a sexual rebel. Perhaps those are some of the reasons he fell in love with me. I know I fell in love with him because he was kind and gentle and funny, because he respected my desires for autonomy and self-fulfillment, and because he loved foreign films, and pizza, and philosophy, and because he was going to become a doctor, and because he wasn't daunted by what I used to call "my crazy family," which included my grandmother, who used to shine a flashlight out the window into any car parked outside our house that contained me and the whichever guy who had driven me home. (She had my best interests in mind: She didn't want me to get pregnant, disgrace the family, enrage my father. At the time, though, it put a serious damper on my love life. Ernie's simple and common-sense solution to my dilemma? To park somewhere else and avoid the histrionics.)

After our marriage, I quickly became staid and settled and enormously responsible. More interested in pot roast than passion. Someone other than the spitfire my husband had married, the free-spirited young woman who had attracted him in the first place.

The woman I lost was the woman he wanted. Though he *seemed* unfaithful to me, paradoxically, he was faithful. To the spirit of the woman he married, to the kind of union he had imagined.

In the months after Ernie's affair, I knew I wanted to concentrate on learning about my own desires, and on starting to fulfill them, so that if our marriage ended, I would not have sacrificed myself and my ambitions for it.

I learned about the kind of marriage I wanted while I was in graduate school, when I started reading about

Virginia Woolf's life. Woolf believed that society's treatment of women, even society itself, could change if individual women made changes in the way they lived their private lives.

Making changes in my marriage meant that my work and his work were considered equally important. Making changes meant sharing everything—decision making, child care, cleaning, cooking, financial responsibility—the works. Our marriage became a work-in-progress in which we would strive to achieve these ideals. I insisted; he was willing. If he hadn't been, our marriage might have ended.

This idea of a flexible marriage demands what many people say they want, but really can't handle: intense, ongoing engagement. Because in a partnership such as the one we have evolved, everything is negotiated and ongoing communication is necessary. Disagreements, arguments, and compromises are daily events. We constantly talk about what we must do if we are to be genuinely faithful to our working partnership.

Some outsiders witnessing this think it's dysfunctional. A well-oiled relationship, to them, is two people agreeing most of the time. This only happens, I believe, when one person (usually the woman) buries her soul and dampens her desire.

Sometimes, even I envy these quiet seemingly

serene relationships. Usually, in time, though, they end. Mine, instead, has persisted.

Ours is a changeable marriage that makes many people nervous. Most people want marriages to be predictable; they want marriages to remain the same. They want to know who cooks, who cleans, who writes the checks, who takes care of the kids.

Far simpler, perhaps, though to me, less enriching, to commit to a more traditional marriage in which roles are fixed than to be engaged in continual flux. Easier to be in a marriage in which sexual fidelity is a certainty, rather than a possibility or a likelihood.

But complexity brings its own rewards. One of them is a sustaining interest in the marriage.

Most people, though, look to marriage as a haven from the world. They don't want marriages to be as thorny, as complicated, and as challenging as the workaday world. (They also, it seems to me, often don't want their marriages to be as much fun.) Trouble is, the workaday world, as everyone who is honest about it will tell you, is a very sexy place to be, and it's erotic because it's so challenging.

It seems to me that if we want to recapture eros in our marriages, we must make them more complex affairs than they usually are. We must allow them (even invite them) to change, to evolve through time, to accommodate us and our ever-changing moods and need for intimacy, to our ever-changing selves.

If we change partners each time we want to reinvent ourselves, we will consume an enormous amount of psychic and emotional energy in separating from one person and mating with another—energy that we might better use for other purposes. The most polygamous people I know are those who, through the years, have grown the least. Though they've changed partners, they themselves have remained the same.

For me, the rewards for staying in a changing marriage are boundless. My relationship, for example, is constantly surprising. For in my thirty-five years of marriage, I've had many different kinds of unions. Some, remote. Others, intimate. Some, deeply satisfying. Others, not so terrific (and, sometimes, for a few years at a stretch).

The marriage I am now in is satisfying, though difficult. I want to work less, play more, and be with him more. He wants to work more—his work now excites him—which means he'll be playing less. This is an about-face for us, because usually I'm the one engulfed in a writing project, unwilling to travel spontaneously, unable to take a Wednesday off for a spontaneous museum trip. After years of supporting my rigid work habits, I'm now asked to accommodate his (and I'm not happy about it).

What to do, what to do, we ask ourselves in the evenings after we've shared the cooking of a special meal (pasta with roasted figs and garlicky baby spinach, for example)? How to maintain our intimacy, our special time together? How to allow him to pursue his desire? How to decide what I must now do to satisfy myself?

The answers, right now, aren't entirely clear to me. I might travel alone; might take my grandson on more excursions; might learn how to make quilts; might improve my bread baking. But I'll figure it out. So will he.

And so it goes. Day by day. Meal by meal. Moment by moment.

After Ernie's affair, what I decided I wanted in my marriage was a secure enough relationship within which to do my work, to raise our children well, but one in which I retained my right to privacy, solitude, independence, and autonomy. I discovered that I preferred loyalty to our ongoing working partnership than a commitment to an uncompromising sexual fidelity. I didn't mind sexual infidelity, if I didn't know about it. (This was before the AIDS epidemic.)

What Ernie wanted from me was support for his choice to change careers whenever he chose, despite the risks involved, with no pressure from me to maintain a certain standard of living, though he assured me he wouldn't jeopardize our well-being, and a promise that I would share responsibility for our income. If he shopped for food, cleaned the house, raised the children with me, he couldn't also be expected to earn our keep. From me, he also wanted unwavering, uncritical support, loyalty, a traveling companion, a conversation partner, passion, humor, and, most important, a commitment to my goals and my life so that he didn't feel as if I needed him to satisfy all my needs.

Whether he wanted my sexual fidelity, I never asked him and he never told me.

I believe that our culture forces us to think negatively about adultery because it threatens the status quo. Adultery always involves risk, change, autonomy. As experience showed me, any encounter with adultery forces us to enter uncharted, and often unpredictable, emotional terrain for all concerned. We become (our partner becomes) someone different.

Because adultery is the enemy of the predictable, settled life, but the ally of change, I believe there are valuable lessons in honoring its impulse, though we may choose not to become unfaithful. (And in an age of AIDS, irresponsible adultery can be a death sentence for us; can be a murderous act toward our partner.)

But what is this impulse to adultery telling us that we need to know even if we choose not to heed it?

Once, when I was writing a novel about adultery, I interviewed a score of married people having affairs. A man, who longed to travel alone, had a lover who lived three hours away. A woman, who wanted to become a famous biographer, became the lover of the world's foremost authority on her subject. Another woman yearned to be a painter; her lover was a street musician.

Without realizing it, these people had found themselves lovers who embodied their unfulfilled dreams. Though they believed their adulteries were giving them something their marriages couldn't, I believe their infidelity replaced more significant change. It was less transgressive to their idea of who they should be in their marriages to, say, travel long distances to see a lover than to journey someplace alone; to sleep with someone important than to try to become important; to spend stolen hours with a musician than to use that time to create. To them, adultery rewrote the unacceptably constraining script of marriage. To me, adultery substituted one constraining script for another.

Their lovers uncannily revealed the secret yearnings of their hearts, the unrealized longings of their souls that requested fulfillment, but that were still thwarted. Years later these people are still filled with desire and regret. They've had their affairs, but they haven't yet satisfied themselves.

I have come to see the impulse toward adultery as the self's yearning to realize its latent potential, as the self's desire to expand itself into uncharted terrain.

I see adultery as the soul's desire to be something other than staid and stable and the heart's desire to yield to ecstasy.

Perhaps if we truly understand the nature of our frustrated desires, and satisfy them, we will not need to stray. And if we do, and if our partners do, we can perhaps take the time to understand why, and in doing so, find wisdom and grace in the process.

Five

One balmy recent October afternoon, I met a man at Canio's in Sag Harbor, my favorite bookshop, where, for whatever reason, I was browsing for more (even more) books about adultery, though my project was drawing to a close.

Canio, the proprietor of the store and a good friend of mine, who makes a point of introducing people he thinks might have common reading interests or common life interests or common cooking interests, grabbed my hand. And he pulled me over to a very tall, very handsome, very curly-headed young man who was balancing a stack of books in both his hands.

"Louise," he said, "I have someone I want you to meet. He's Italian and he'll be here just a few more days."

Canio introduces me to Fabio ("such a beautiful name," Canio says), who runs a waterfront restaurant in Italy's Lake District during the summer months, and who spends the rest of his time traveling.

Not a bad life, I think to myself. The restaurant, Fabio tells me, specializes in pizzas and pastas, and I say how delightful I think it would be to have a simple meal in such a setting. And soon we are sharing memories of our favorite meals, our favorite pastas, our favorite pizzas.

"Spaghetti with the smallest clams you can imagine, clams as tiny as the fingernail on your little finger," Fabio says. "With garlic, fresh garlic, just picked from the earth, and a lovely light olive oil, recently pressed." He kisses the tips of his fingers and looks deep into my eyes in the way that Italian men do when they're talking about food and when they're talking to a woman, even if that woman is far older than they are.

"Pizza with caramelized onions, smoked mozzarella, and fresh thyme," I respond, looking deep into Fabio's eyes in the way that Italian-American women do when they're talking to a gorgeous young man who reminds them of their sons and of their past. And I ask Fabio for the address of his restaurant, and I tell him that I want to visit it, that I will visit it, the next time I travel to Italy.

In another time, in another place, in another life, in another narrative, Fabio and I might have become lovers and the story that I have to tell about adultery might have changed thereby. But the end of our story—Fabio's and mine, for we do have a story, although it is a very short one—and the end of this narrative, is, I think, far more interesting than any adulterous love affair we might have shared. For I know that though it might have brought me much pleasure, it surely, too, would have entailed more sorrow than I now am willing to experience.

"She's a writer," Canio tells Fabio as he brushes by, in search of a biography of Queen Elizabeth for another customer. "Tell him what you're writing."

Reluctantly, I tell Fabio that I am writing a book about adultery. He blushes. I blush. He looks down. I look down. He is, I can tell, very well bred and, though our conversation has come easily until this moment, he doesn't now know what to say. And I can't blame him. For what does one say to a woman one has just met who tells you that she is writing a book about adultery?

So I quickly sketch something about my work, and I make it sound terribly literary, and Fabio, relieved, smiles again. But then I tell him something about the part about my grandfather, and about where he comes from, and what I have imagined of his past.

Fabio nods. He tells me that, yes, he knows that part of Italy, that, yes, he too has heard that the people of that region commonly have lovers.

He pauses. He blushes, and says, "But, Louise, that can be said about any region of Italy, and about any part of the world, about America, even."

I laugh, for of course it is true.

"But, in the book, do you talk about yourself as well?" Fabio asks me. He is very serious about this.

"Somewhat," I say. I surely do not want to share with this stranger my adultery story. I do not want to tell him that, even now, women who tell their adultery stories seriously endanger their marriages. That, for this reason, I have deliberately chosen not to write forthrightly about my life in this way. Because if I admit that I've had an affair, or two, or more, it would risk my marriage. But if I admit I haven't, it would seem that I upheld a double standard for women and men in these matters, which I don't.

"I talk about what might have happened to me, not what actually happened to me," I say evasively.

I tell Fabio, too, that I relate my husband's story, and I quickly describe that critical event in our lives.

"You and your husband," Fabio asks hesitantly. "Are you still married?"

"Oh yes," I reply. "Married, now, some thirty-six years. And with two grown sons, a grandson, and another grandbaby on the way, a girl."

"Ah." Fabio smiles. He seems relieved. For although adultery plots may fascinate Italians, those that entail the breakup of a marriage, I have found, invariably leave them in despair. "Then I have a book that you must both read. Please allow me to buy it for you, to commemorate our meeting."

Fabio pulls me over to a revolving bookstand and he selects a slim paperbound volume. *Silk,* a novel by Alessandro Baricco. He buys it, and hands it to me with a flourish.

"This," Fabio says, "you must read. It will explain much." He tells me how, when the work is published in Italy in 1996 as *Seta,* it becomes a best-seller because it so elegantly expresses what Italians believe about the nature of adultery, and about love and fidelity.

"It is a beautiful story," he says. "It is a tragic story. But it is beautiful and tragic in ways that you cannot possibly expect, and I promise that, more than any other novel about adultery you've read, it will be the most significant. It might remind you of something you might have already discovered, but it will tell you something that is, nonetheless, worth remembering."

The story begins with a gossamer silk scarf, the color of sunset (like the one I imagine my grandfather giving his lover as a present), and the dream of a man named Baldiabiou to transform the tiny village of Lavilledieu in France into a prosperous center for the production of silk for garments as magnificent as that scarf.

The hero is a dapper young silkworm trader named

Herve Joncour whom Baldiabiou persuades to travel to the farthest corners of the earth in search of healthy silkworm eggs after an epidemic has destroyed those from European hatcheries.

Baldiabiou decides that Joncour must travel to Japan, for he has once held in his hand a veil woven from Japanese silk thread so fine that holding the veil felt like holding nothing at all. The difficulties are in getting to Japan, in finding someone with whom to trade, and in smuggling the eggs from Japan, for doing so was a criminal offense.

Nevertheless, Joncour goes, for he believes it is his destiny. He says good-bye to his wife, Helene, a tall woman with long black hair and a most beautiful voice. And he tells her not to worry about him, that he will return to her safely.

In Japan, Joncour meets Hara Kei, a man willing to do business with him. And he sees a young woman with the face of a young girl who seems to be European. She rests her head in Hara Kei's lap and it seems that she is his concubine. She opens her eyes and looks at Joncour intensely as he explains who he is and what he wants. But the woman's attention is unsettling and provocative.

As Joncour watches her, she slips her hand from her kimono; she lifts her head; she sips tea. She continues to watch Joncour. And her look is enough to change the shape of his life forever.

Louise DeSalvo *Adultery*

He returns, though, to Lavilledieu, bringing his wife Helene the present of a sheer tunic which her modesty will not allow her to wear. Still, his marriage to Helene suffers for his love for her can't compare with the obsession he develops for this elusive woman with the face of a girl whom he has seen for those few moments in Japan.

Joncour travels again to Japan, and again, and again. More for the hope of seeing this woman than for reasons of commerce. And he sees her again, and perhaps encounters her, though he can't be certain, when he is blindfolded during a ritual bath, and a woman whom he can't see washes him and caresses him with a silk cloth.

While he is still blindfolded, she gives him a tiny scrap of paper with an inked message in Japanese ideograms. The message, which is later translated for him by a Japanese brothel-owner in France, reads, "Come back, or I shall die."

So, of course, he returns. And he sees her again. This time, though, she offers him another woman as lover, a present, apparently, from Hara Kei. And he makes love to this other woman, and not to her, though he thinks of her, as he makes love to this other woman, so it is almost like making love to her.

On a later visit to Japan, all is changed for Japan is in the midst of civil war and Hara Kei's village has been destroyed and his people are in flight. A boy who shows Joncour to Hara Kei's encampment is killed because Hara Kei knows the woman has sent for Joncour. So Joncour must leave and he can never return. And so he leaves. Through all these years, he has never been alone with this woman who has obsessed him, for whom he's risked so much, and for whom he's sacrificed the happiness of his marriage.

One day, some months after his return home, Joncour gets a letter written in Japanese. It is from her, he believes. He goes to Nîmes to have it translated.

It is an exquisite, long, loving, and erotic letter, with explicit instructions for a night of love.

> *Stay like this,* the letter reads, *I want to look at you, I have looked at you so much but you were not for me, now you are for me, don't come close, please, stay as you are, we have a night to ourselves, and I want to look at you, I've never seen you in this way, your body for me, your skin, shut your eyes. . . .*
>
> *Who will ever be able to erase this moment that is happening? and this body of mine no longer with any silk, your hands touching it, your eyes looking at it. . .*
>
> *Preserve your life out of my reach. And do not for a moment hesitate, should it be useful for your happiness, to forget this woman who now says to you, without regret, farewell.*

In the years that follow, Joncour and his wife Helene live tranquilly in Lavilledieu and are surprised at finding much happiness (though no erotic life) in each other's company. At times, though, Joncour dreams of his phantom love.

On the day that Baldiabiou moves from Lavilledieu forever, Joncour watches Helene cry and embrace Baldiabiou passionately in public. Joncour thinks that, when he himself has departed for Japan, his wife has never embraced him in this way; she has never cried.

After Helene's death, and through a strange set of circumstances, Joncour discovers something astonishing and tragic. For he learns that the passionate letter describing the imaginary night of lovemaking he thought was penned by the woman he met in Japan was, in truth, written by his wife. She has had it translated into Japanese, and delivered to their home.

But what can this mean? Joncour wonders. That Helene knew the substance of his longings? That she understood them? That she cared so deeply about him that she wrote him this letter?

But where had Helene learned the art of erotic love? And why didn't he understand that she knew its secrets? Was Helene capable of an erotic life that Joncour couldn't ever imagine, and so, in loving this far-off woman, he has foreclosed the possibility of the passionate, erotic love of his wife?

There is much that Joncour can never know. But now, near the end of his life, Joncour does know this. That in pursuing a phantom, he has forever lost the experience of loving his wife, the most erotic woman he could ever have known.

Ernie and I lie in bed together. I have just finished reading *Silk,* and I am telling him its ending, which has made me cry. When Ernie hears it, he cries too, and embraces me. He tells me he's glad he's not Herve Joncour. I tell him I'm happy I'm not Helene. I say I think it's the most exquisite fable about the experience of adultery that I've ever read.

"What do you mean?" he asks. "How can you know? You've never been unfaithful."

"I just know," I answer, "from everything I've read, from everything I've learned."

The day after I finish reading *Silk,* I go to Canio's, for I want to find out where Fabio is staying so that I can thank him, so that I can talk to him about the novel. But Canio tells me that I'm too late, that Fabio has already left for Italy.

Although Canio does not tell me anything about Fabio's departure, I see him taking the train into New York City, making his way down to the docks, and finding a boat that will take him back Italy. It will be months before the restaurant opens, and Fabio has